THOMAS MARCOTTY

Dagger Blessing

The Tibetan Phurpa Cult: Reflections and Materials

B.R. PUBLISHING CORPORATION
Delhi-110052

ISBN 81-7018-411-8

Published by Pradeep Mittal for B.R. Publishing Corporation at 461, Vivekanand Nagar, Delhi-110052.
Distributed by D.K. Publishers' Distributors at 1, Ansari Road, Darya Ganj, New Delhi-110002. Phone 278368. Printed at D.K. Fine Art Press, Delhi.

PRINTED IN INDIA

Contents

DOGMATICS:

Questions and Answers

1. In the Tibetan texts describing the details of the Phurpa-cult (cult of the Tibetan ritual dagger) it is unequivocally said (Ratna-glin-pa; Kanjur, Vol. 10, "Vajramantra...") that demons have to be killed (bsad) by the Phurpa practitioner. The first question is, therefore, if this practice is in accordance with Lord Buddha's teachings who - also unequivocally - forbids the killing of sentient beings?

2. In the mentioned texts the word "kill" (bsad) is here and there replaced by the word "liberate" (sgrol) and it is supposed to mean that an evil sentient being is transfered to a better existence by ritually murdering it. So the second question is: Is there any difference between "killing" and "liberating" and, if yes, how can this difference be described?

3. It is maintained by Phurpa practitioners that liberating or killing evil sentient beings (demons) is an act of "Special Compassion" and that this special compassion can justify an offence against Lord Buddha's rule. Third question: a) Is there a "Special Compassion" justifying ritual murder (sgrol-ba)? b) How can a person acquire this special compassion?

4. It is maintained that only those sentient beings are killed or liberated (by Phurpa) who are obsessed by the evil. So the fourth question is how the evil must be defined nowadays? It should be mentioned that in former times (in the context of the ritual murder of King Glan-dar-ma committed by a Buddhist) the evil was defined as the rejection (suppression) of Dharma. If this definition would be maintained today a peaceful coexistence of Tibetan Buddhists and those who have rejected Buddhism (e.g. Swiss or American citizens) would be impossible. So the fourth question is: What is the definition of the evil?

5. The Phurpa cult is widely practiced also today. The Dalai Lamas have, in the past, never rejected the theory of allowed ritual murder (the Phurpa cult). His Holiness, the 14. Dalai Lama, has a Phurpa priest in his entourage. Can it, therefore, be correct to say that his Holiness agrees with the Phurpa practitioners?

ཀ། ཆོས་འཁོར་དགོན།

TIBETAN INSTITUTE CH-8486 RIKON/ZH TEL. 052 35 17 29 P.C. 84-5934 WINTERTHUR

Rikon, March 4, 1986

Dear Mr. Marcotty,

thank you for your letter dated February 26. I have presented your questions to the community of monks and the Abbot has answered them in Tibetan. Ladrö Rinpoche has then retranslated the answers into German.

Question 1: All beings of the six spheres of existence lastly are sentient beings. They all deserve our compassion. In case that a demon is ritually 'killed' he is killed for compassion. And now an important point: Not the demon himself is killed. Only his bad qualities are destroyed, the demon being freed of these bad qualities afterwards.

Question 2: For this reason in the Tibetan texts the word 'sgrol' (liberate) is frequently used and not 'bsad' (kill).

Question 3: The priest needs a very special concentration (Special Compassion) in order not to hurt the sentient being. He only kills its bad qualities. Would he not succeed so far, the ritual murder would amount to common murder followed by very serious karmic consequences.

Question 4: The definition of the evil has never changed. It is the three poisons: ignorance, hatred and lust. The Abbot, after some reflection, added the following legend: 'Lord Buddha, in one of his former incarnations, once killed a black magician who intended to murder 500 merchants. This way Lord Buddha not only saved the lives of the merchants. He also averted a terrible Karma from the magician. But also in this case Lord Buddha only destroyed the magician's bad qualities: his hatred and lust, both born from ignorance. Buddha did all this with Special Compassion and thus acquired great Merits'.

Question 5: His Holiness recognizes the Phurpa Cult though he himself does not practice it.

Being always glad to hear from you I remain

Yours faithfully

Peter Grieder

THOMAS MARCOTTY

On the Phurpa Cult

The Quantities of Happiness

Sooner or later we all tend to wonder, why times of bliss should be so rare in our lives. Many people among us spend their life mainly in a state of emotional uneasiness the intensness of which may occasionally increase or decrease; yet rarely, too seldomly anyway, does it give way to a state of mind one might unreservedly call happy: too many people are too often unhappy. And upon inquiring into the reasons one will not obtain a sensible answer. Luck has simply deserted them for no apparent cause or reason. They are at odds with themselves and not open to any reasoning or argument.

This lack of subjectively experienced bliss, hence the unhappiness, is a widespread disease. Only about one third of the people living in Central Europe consider themselves generally happy. Another third are more or less infested with the germ of emotional uneasiness, the remaining third describing themselves as outright unhappy. This information may be derived from systematic studies (1) which all lead to the same or at least very similar results, namely to this one-third-parity.

These studies, however, do not represent mere juggling with figures: society - the nations and their institutions - may not bear the entire responsability for the happiness of its members according to modern thinking, though it definitely has a share in it. That is why many governments make certain limited funds available for the sporadic enquiry into their voters' well-being. Thanks to this mainly government financed happiness research we have a fairly good knowledge of this subject. And what do the results of such studies teach us?

From these studies it appears that happiness is partly a subjective emotion but partly also the consequence of objective factors. It is a known fact that German civil servants are, for instance, in general happier people than others: they have sufficient room for self-realization, yet they enjoy simultaneously being provided for which in turn further adds to their happiness. By international comparison the US Americans are ranking right on top

Head of a Phurpa dagger.

of the scale of the happy: in the United States social norm has it that being happy is a civil duty. And this is what it results in: approximately one half of the North Americans interviewed declare themselves happy and only a few people are willing openly to profess their subjective unhappiness when asked.

Now, such taboos are not valid for Europe and much less so for Asia where even movies must invariably finish with an unhappy ending if they are to make money. The proportion of people in Asia calling themselves happy decreases significantly, occasionally going down to under ten percent. On the whole one must assume the number of unhappy people on this globe to be rather large and this also in countries where the sources of conventional ill-luck - disease, famine, and war - have largely dried up: About fifteen millions grown-up Federal Germans, a million and a half grown-up Swiss. How many millions of grown-up Indians? One had better not ask children. And this is what this book is about: is there anything we can do to spend the limited life-time allotted to us in a happier way? Let me tell you the answer at this stage already: yes, one can do something to increase happiness. People have thought about it and acted in different ways. In this context one finds quite interesting attempts and examples and one of these great attempts is and has been the Tibetan dagger cult.

A Precept of Bliss

The dagger cult is a precept of bliss. Maybe the reader of these lines will never have heard of this cult before. And there is no reason to reproach yourself with it. Others, including myself, are in the same position. My first confrontation with the bliss producing dagger occured rather accidentally at the time: in Ashok Mehra's shop. Ashok Mehra, originally a Kashimiri, is one of the great art dealers of Delhi. In his shop the foreign traveller could, at least then, admire the treasures of Asia: rubies arranged according to size and colour and displayed on black velvet trays, bronze statues from the Swat valley, and Tibetan altar silver. It was there that, more out of curiosity than connoisseurship, I purchased a ritual dagger, a 'Phurpa' (2) as you may see it on the picture: an iron knife with a three-edged blade and a bronze hilt decorated with faces and signs.

Back in Europe I at first tried the great libraries in order to find information on the use of such daggers, the way of handling them, and what kind of people employ Phurpas. The result I obtained was rather unsatisfactory. These daggers are mentioned here and there; indeed, one does find the book by an American (3) on the iconography of ritual daggers. Yet no scholar of the Himalayas has reported anything in detail. None has ever witnessed a Phurpa ceremony or taken photographs of such ritual. Also my enquiries with Tibetan lamas living in Europe as refugees initially remained without almost any tangible result. Only the contours of an ancient and apparently highly developed cult emerged.

Tibetan ritual dagger.

In the years following I again travelled to India, to Sikkim, and Nepal and had tea there with strange people, searched around in temples, ventured on sometimes adventurous tours in jeeps and taxis, and compiled one notebook after the other. I collected pictures, took photographs myself and - this turning out to be of importance - traced some old scriptures on the Phurpa cult though not in Asia by the way. On the contrary, this was almost around the corner, in the library of the Musée Guimet in Paris and in the external stores of the university library at Tübingen. These texts, written in Tibetan, I have had translated. This brought me a step further. The provisional result consisted of a number of cardboard boxes full of photographs, slides, daggers, loose notes, translated texts, offering cups, silk rags, mustard seeds, and all sorts of bits and pieces that belong to the Phurpa cult. Putting these parts and particles together an initially blurred and then quite clear picture emerges. To my own surprise this picture disclosed a precept, an instruction manual for bliss or to achieve happiness.

Extension of the Dagger Cult

This doctrine is over a thousand years old yet, despite its advanced age, it remains largely understandable to twentieth century readers. The immediacy and liveliness with which the authors of the original texts attached to this book speak to us over this vast historical distance has astonsihed me time and again. But one should also beware of errors: the dagger cult as well as the pertinent texts date from an era where science, religion, and magic were still forming a unity. This venerable unity - and this is the problem - got lost in Europe in the course of past centuries. Religion and science have seperated and developed independently. Magic has been declared illegitimate. Hence the reader may consequently wonder whether I e.g., the reporter, am secretly indulging in magic like Doctor Faustus once upon a time. In this context I might add a little explanatory story: I have a respected friend who has, studied indology occupying himself all his life with research into Buddhism and mainly with the historical Buddha figure at that. It is, therefore, no wonder that people occasionally ask him whether he himself is meditating every day prostrating in front of a Buddha image and if he was a believer in Buddhism? He likes to reply by the counter-question: whether an ornithologist, a professional bird-watcher, must necessarily be able to lay eggs? The dagger cult and its magical aspect is a similar matter. With all due respect to the subject one ought not necessarily want to lay eggs too.

With regard to the strangeness of the subject certain questions to its presentation arise: how can one acquaint today's readers with such a subject-matter over the times without distorting it? This questions has been answered as follows on the following pages: at first the dagger cult will be described by an occidental to western readers. Hence the contents habe been passed through the sieve of western ideas making it easier to understand. But in the course of this procedure the subject, the dagger cult, looses its particular fragrance. That is why this first part will be followed by a second part where the adherents of the Phurpa cult will have their direct say. In these Tibetan text originals the master is adressing the pupil, the old dagger priest the young, the stranger is speaking to the stranger. An occidental reader might find it difficult to follow the teaching of the beatifying dagger in its original form. But in reading it he will be confronted with the entire dagger world unfiltered and in all its peculiarity and beauty.

Here there is some information on the area and the time of the dagger cult: imagine a map of Asia and marked on it a triangle the bases line of which runs from Delhi to Hong Kong. The right-hand and roughly perpendicular side of the triangle extends from Hong Kong to Tokyo and the third or left side runs from Tokyo back to Delhi in a curve including Mongolia. Within this triangle embracing parts of India, Nepal, Bhutan, China, Japan, Korea, and Russia, the dagger cult was or still is at home, al-

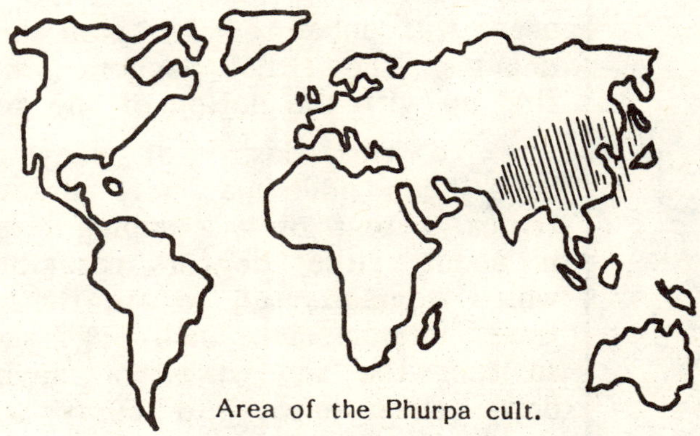

Area of the Phurpa cult.

though with a number of restrictions: regarding Japan (5) all we know is that the dagger cult does exist. However, no details have become known so far. Mongolia and China, including Tibet, are now marxist people's republics. That is why it is not known precisely to what extent the dagger cult is still practised there. Anyway, we are speaking of a huge area comparable to the surface of the United States of America. So much for the geography of the Phurpa cult.

Anybody who has been dealing with Buddhism will now notice that the area of the Phurpa cult is practically identical with that of Mahayana Buddhism, also called the 'Great Vehicle'. This leads to the assumption that the teaching of the dagger might be an offshoot of Mahayana Buddhism if not part of it. This is corroborated by the following fact: nowadays the Phurpa cult is practised mainly by Buddhist monks, principally by the members of the Nyingmapa order or 'red caps'. They are the non-reformist monks who remained faithful to the 'teachings of the old' contrary to the 'yellow caps', reformists who rather reject the dagger cult. Yet this appearance may be misleading. Judging by the present state of knowledge one may also presume that the Phurpa cult and Mahayana Buddhism coexist by mere coincidence in the same region: the Phurpa cult, examples for this can be found (6), can very well do without Buddhism. On the other hand the Buddhists are not dependant upon the dagger cult. And history, profane as well as divine, even allows the supposition that the Phurpa cult and the teachings of Gautama Buddha originate from quite different times and cultures.

Sumerian Origin?

First the profane history: by this I mean history in the western scientific sense of the word. According to this the dagger cult is at least a thousand years older than Buddhism. The first traces of the Phurpa cult are not even to be found in the Buddhist sphere of influence. The earliest ritual daggers are rather to be found in Mesopotamia, now Irak, where they have been discovered among the relics of Sumerian times. The Sumerian daggers, this is what we do know, served for the so-called soil consecration. This means they were driven into the ground as a kind of border markings to indicate to everybody, mainly the roaming demons, that the thus marked and bordered area was inhabited by man and thus out of bounds to demons. The ritual daggers are right from the beginning tied up with the notion of the defense of demons (7).

To this desire of denying access to demons may have been added a more practical purpose. Anyone who struck a tent on a camping site will now know what this is about: ritual daggers resemble the pegs by the aid of which nomads used to tie their tents to the ground from times immemorial. Such pegs should best be made of iron so that the tent dwellers maybe in a better position to drive them also into stony soil. Furthermore the pegs should be shaped three-edged to avoid the wind and weather pulling them out. And thus we obtain the principal characteristics that mark the Phurpa up to this day: ritual daggers ought to be forged of iron their blades having three edges (8). All these are features that have no relation to Buddhism whatsoever.

This much is to be said for the profane history. In addition to that there is the divine history mainly written down by Buddhist monks which leads to a similar result, if by different means. It begins with a legend from the 8th century A.D. which seems touching to modern observers: the Tibetans who were then known to be nomad cattle herdsmen, dreaded as robbers, are according to the legend supposed to have come to the understanding that they, the dwellers on the roof of the world, are actually wicked barbarians. Endeavouring to achieve a more refined way of life and to follow the example of their neighbours, the ever-so-civilized Indians and Chinese, their then king Thi-srong-de-tsen invited Indian sages into the country who were to tell the Tibetan people the teaching of Gautama Buddha.

One of these sages, by the name of Padmasambhava, is today regarded as the founder of Tibetan Buddhism. In his biography (9) one can read that Padmasambhava is said to have 'discovered' the dagger cult on his way to Tibet, actually he is supposed to have found the dagger precept in a cave. The doctrine of the beatifying dagger, meaning the ritual scriptures as reproduced in this book, lay there hidden in a triangular stone receptacle guarded by a large scorpion. I ought to mention at this juncture that there are certainly thousands of caves in the Himalayas and among them one which might as well have been the scene of the event. I visited it once. It is a low cre-

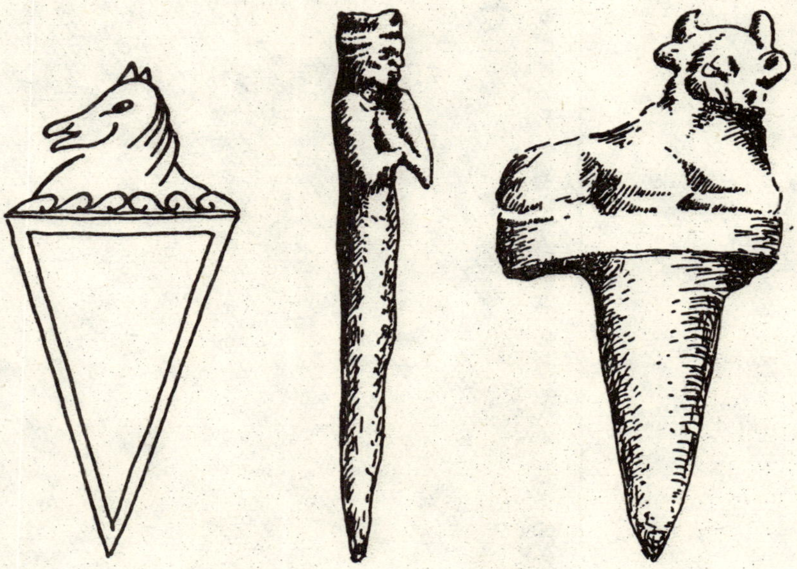

Sumerian ritual daggers (after S. Hummel).

vasse in the rocks of a mountain, near the Nepalese village of Pharping. One can only walk in it stooped. At present the cave is inhabited by a friendly monk practising a moderate form of the Phurpa cult there. The cave is furnished with rugs and electric light. We had buttered tea in there discussing dagger problems by the aid of an interpreter, even exchanging ritual daggers in the end. I gave him my dagger for which I got his much to my enjoyment.

Indian Origin?

Back now to Padmasambhava: the holy man from India, also known by the name of Guru Rinpoche, has obviously not brought the dagger cult from his southern homeland but came upon it in the Himalayas. Another place in the text (10) points to this too. Here it says Padmasambhava had 'perfected' the Phurpa cult which again implies the existence of the dagger cult before the appearance of the guru. It is by the way unknown, which contribution Padmasambhava made to the perfection of the cult. The dagger followers practising today however stick mostly to texts of which they do themselves explicit-

Padmasambhava (car stickers for the propagation of Vajrayana Buddhism in Europe).

ly declare that they go back at least partially to Guru Rinpoche. This leads us to the assumption that the cult had already been developed in its basic form (retained up to this day) as early as in the 8th century.

Treasure Texts Rediscovered

What such original texts look like you may see on the photo. It shows the section of a page of the handwritten manuscript photocopied from a dagger magician's handbook, the original going back to about 1450 A.D. The 472 page volume, originally written on strips, bears the title 'Most secret rites for the invocation of the (dagger god) Phurpa for destructive purposes'. This text was written down by a Tibetan writer by the name of Ratna-glin-pa. Ratna-glin-pa is however not the actual author as is mentioned in the colophones of the various sections: The authorship is mostly attributed to Padmasambhava (8th century) who is said to have composed the 'treasure texts' hiding them in caves until man will have become worthy of this secret teaching. There they were then 'rediscovered' by Ratna-glin-pa in the 15th century. Who knows to what extent one is to take this history word-for-word? However, it furnishes yet another hint that the originally Sumerian tent peg had already then, at the time of Charlemagne, developed into the focal point of an individual cult which has survived under the protection and in the shadow of a tolerant host religion, Buddhism, right into our days (11).

In the course of my dagger studies I sometimes asked myself why there should be no coherent treatise on the Phurpa cult in the western literature as yet in spite of the cult's obviously considerable expansion. In the meantime I have gained some experience myself and I think I now know why the dagger cult has escaped the Tibet scholars. There are three main reasons for that: In the

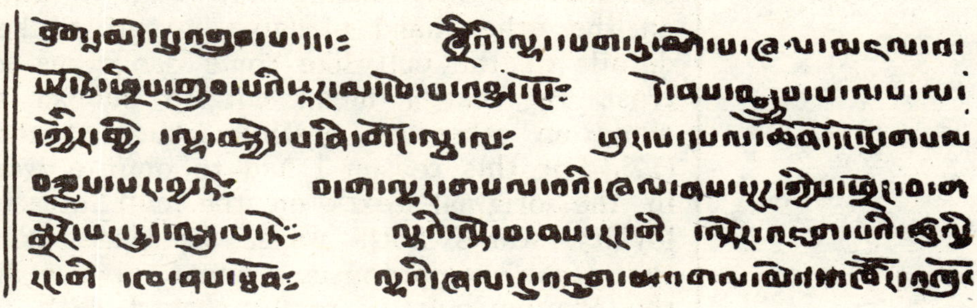

Part of a Tibetan manuscript.

first place mention must be made of the peculiar Zeitgeist of past epochs: The early Tibet travellers of the 18th and 19th century had other things to worry about. They were above all missionaries who in the land of Buddhas and daggers, if one is to believe their own reports, hardly succeeded in saving any souls at all and who kept their attention fixed to the obvious, i.e. Buddhism, and not to the dagger cult flourishing in hiding.

It was not much different with the 19th century 'explorers' following in their footsteps. They were Russian and in particular British professional agents, often trained by H.M. Secret Service in the north Indian Dhera Dun military academy who, disguised in all sorts of fashions, had to reconnoitre which powers might exert an influence on Tibet potentially threatening the one-time colony of British India from the north. Naturally these explorers were only interested in Tibet, its probablea mineral resources, and the value of this country as a military deployment bases and not so much in the Tibetans and their 'idolatry' as it is sometimes called in their reports to the high command at Calcutta.

The second obstacle to the research into the dagger cult appears to be an imbalance of interest in what the adherents of other cultures think and do. We find it quite normal and correct to travel to foreign countries and to get to know the objects of our curiosity, to photograph and to document them. Our Asian friends however do not feel this urge, at least not to this degree. In the sphere of the dagger cult, not to speak of other problem fields, this results in a misunderstanding which surely also confronted my predecessors in the search for the dagger truth: an initiated dagger practitioner, let us say in Nepal, simply cannot imagine that his visitor from the far-away west earnestly desires to learn something about the Phurpa cult but shows no visible intention of really exercising it. In other words, here again emerges the problem of the ornithologist who does not desire to lay eggs, but this time in a different perspective.

Such misunderstandings however can often be bridged once you lay them quite open over the usual cup of tea. A compromise will then be within easy reach. It usually amounts to my finding out what I want to know while on the other hand pledging myself to keep secret certain details of the cult like some dangerous magic spells (mantras). By that I mean not to publish them in order to avoid an otherwise possible abuse of the Phurpa doctrine (12). For this reason I had to omit a word here and there in the original texts on the cult attached to this book: loyalty works both ways. There is no denying, though, that such compromises cannot always be brought about: the Phurpa cult is really soaked with fear and mistrust. That is why tea might occasionally also finish with cool reciprocal disappointment.

Language Barriers

The third obstacle familiar to any traveller to Asia is the language barrier. In the case of the dagger cult it looks like this: the dagger believers speak as their mother tongue Nepali, Lepcha and mainly Tibetan. And these are languages which until very recently were mastered fluently by hardly any westerner. Here one example: when the British entered Tibet with about 3000 troops in 1903 there was only one officer among them who had a fair command of Tibetan (13). And vice versa. The Tibetans were very poor in learning European languages. So the language barrier remained impenetrable for a long while and I personally suspect that this nearly perfect impenetrability might have contributed to producing that highly idealised image of Tibet such as it has emerged in the west since the beginning of this century. The violent dagger cult, and this is quite clear, cannot be discerned on this ideal picture of the land of snow with its saints clad in silk.

The situation only changed with the Chinese invasion in Tibet in the course of the fifties. There was nobody to count them. But it is said that possibly one hundred thousand Tibetans fled their country at the time. The refugees, and in Switzerland alone there live about 2000, have more or less managed to learn the languages of their host countries. I like to remember a geshe, that is a doctor of Buddhist theology, who once translated for me the conversation with a dagger man without faltering from Kham-Tibetan (dialect) into Swiss German (dialect). The more important universities availed themselves of the opportunity at the time to get highly educated clergymen from the refugee camps in India who have since been lecturers teaching students in Europe the Tibetan language and script.

A New Tibetology

The language barrier became more permeable. And with this the Tibet image, hitherto painted in more subdued pastel shades, gained fresh colour. The first book of this revised tibetology was published in 1956. Its author, René de Nebesky-Wojkowitz (14), assisted by Tibetan refugees acting as translators, no longer presented Buddhism as upper class ethics but as a loud and sometimes burlesque demonic and chaotic popular religion in the scope of which even the sublime, Gautama Buddha, plays merely a minor part as Guru Shakyamuni. Buddhism as we thought we knew it figures since as a mere film on hot milk which, as we have now learnt, mainly consists of colorful legends, artful magic, and last but not least the tantric Phurpa cult. By this I do not wish to say that the old elevated picture of Buddhism is a distorted one. It was just a bit incomplete requiring some supplements.

Given the necessary patience and perseverance one can nowadays quite effortless find out, copy, photograph, film and learn everything provided the researcher carries with him the necessary recommendations and knows how to make out the good places where things happen. Among these places advisable to the Phurpa researcher is a small Nepalese town by the name of Bodnath. Near the great stupa one can find a crowded restaurant which is rather an information exchange where sooner or later the dagger adepts will all pass by. Also Gangtok (in Sikkim) and Darjeeling, the old summer resort for British colonial officers, are places where to make a find. Yet the dagger researcher need not travel that far. Already in Rikon, the Tibetan refugee settlement not far from Zürich in Switzerland,

one may with some patience be initiated in the basics of the dagger cult.

I should not forget to mention here that the Phurpa cult, this strange piece of ancient wisdom, is not at all withering away, thus following the example of other cultures so often wasting away in museums. The opposite seems to be correct: on the one side the dagger cult fits so tightly with people's demand for a comprehensible and sensual ritual which there is no reason to discard despite the Buddhist clergy's shaking a warning finger. On the other hand the Phurpa cult is at present even up to little renaissance whose raison d'être are not easy to determine. One sometimes gets the impression that the constant absence of the Buddhist dignitaries - they must nowadays often go and collect donations in Europe and the United States - makes the less learned people turn more frequently to the ritual dagger again.

Happiness here and now

In addition to this there is another attraction: as was hinted before the Phurpa cult is no salvation cum enlightenment dogma comparable to Christianity or Buddhism demanding discipline and sacrifice from their followers. The dagger cult is rather based on the idea of happiness and luck being achievable. It does not intend to deliver people from their sins nor to help them to attain a better status in rebirth. Yet the Phurpa cult does not keep man from these high aims. But it serves the main purpose of turning unhappy people into happy ones, and this not some other time in a life after death, but here and now.

This central thought of the Phurpa cult, the manageability of luck, may surprise occidental readers or seem strange to them. Because 'luck', as you may read in the Brockhaus encyclopaedia, first means as much as chance: luck in roulette gambling, luck as you need it when crossing a busy road. It on the other hand signifies a 'likewise quickly passing as well as rare state of absence of desire'. In both cases it amounts to something like an accidentally granted favour comparable to a sun-ray despite a cloudy sky but nothing that could be systematically achieved. Achievable for us are vaccines against epidemics, dams or eight-lane motorways, anything belonging to the external side of the world that furnishes us with the comforts of life which should not be carelessly disdained. But when looking at the complex of the internal values of our world, one finds the range of what is achievable reduced to a funnel-shaped outlet leading to an apparently invariable uneasiness.

In Asia, especially in Tibet, the situation was and has been ever since the opposite: interference with the external world, things like road construction or mining, were, therefore, a long time considered undesirable, contrary to nature or 'unsuitable for enlightment'. The external living conditions are consequently to this day often unbearable. But forming and mastering the inner world, the imaginative and perceptive power ranks high on top. Pushing

Full iron dagger with silken flag and ritual skullcap.

for a moment the occidental encyclopaedic notion of luck and happiness aside in attempting to reconsider the following three theses, the principle of the manageability of luck, otherwise unusual to us, does become more comprehensible. First of all - this being thesis number one - luck or happiness can be understood as the absence of ill-luck or unhappiness. This definition, which is also for westerners not entirely new (15), proves quite practical in the search of luck: It is difficult to say what luck could possibly be. There are, however, hardly any differences of opinion on the nature of misfortune.

Defining Happiness

The sources of human misfortune are limited in number and recognizable: it all starts with misfortune of an exogenous nature such as war, plague and famine, hence manifestations of misfortune which we Central Europeans mostly know only from television. This is followed by, number two, the regular illnesses and diseases. In the Himalayas these were above all yellow fever, smallpox, and syphilis in consequence of a casual sexual morality which already made the early Christian missionaries frown. Number three and at last there come the mental disorders which may be summarized under the heading of 'meditation obstacles': psychosomatic disorders, concentration weakness, diffuse anxieties, mortal fear, neurosis and psychosis, i.e. endogenous phenomena of misfortune or unhappiness, which as for their intensity and expansion might as well be regarded as the main sources of misfortune in the industrialized countries.

This was the first dogma of luck: luck or happiness is to be defined by the absence of misfortune or unhappiness. The second dogma now says that misfortune of any and all kinds is an illness and a self-inflicted one as that. This thesis does not go down easily. One may object that one could not very well call a person ill because - first version of misfortune - his harvest was ruined by a hailstorm and he will consequently starve. Neither are we prepared to call things like mortal fear, diffuse anxieties and similar meditation obstacles of the third type a misfortune.

Fatalistic Occidentals

There is much to be said in favour of such obejections. But don't such arguments simply hide the clumsy notion according to which luck and ill-luck bear the characteristics of accidentalness? The fatalistic occidental idea of luck which a not precisely determined power is lavishly pouring out of its cornucopia or refusing to do so? If on the contrary you subscribe to the idea of luck being manageable and not accidental then misfortune, too, can not very well be accidental. All this leads to this question: can we accept a wider definition of illness not being limited to sufferings in the medical sense but including misfortune of any kind, even thunderstorms and concentrating deficiencies? Taking this point of view bona fide the logic of this can only be thus: the Nepalese farmer whose harvest is ruined by hail or the person suffering from diffuse anxieties is not in proper order. He is ill.

Full iron Phurpas

Because otherwise he would have had luck and not been up to misfortune. The problem, therefore, is to cure this illness. For that one needs a therapy. And one of these therapeutic methods is the Phurpa cult, the handling of the benedictory dagger.

Before coming to the third dogma of luck I should like to digress for a moment and tell you about an Indian whom I met years ago at a seminar somewhere in Holland. This Indian, a shrewd specialist, has been earning his living in Europe as a professional Guru and a sought-after story teller of Indian fairy tales. We were discussing the question to which extent occidentals are ready to accept things strange and of another kind. He being a specialist thought: the wise man would always move into the foreground what is similar, of the same kind, and what one has in common only spicing his mental food with a dash of oriental strangeness as long as he attaches importance to applause and baksheesh.

One should never disregard the advice of wise men. Yet I must demand the reader at least to examine favourably the somewhat delicate third theorem of luck. It says that the illness of misfortune is caused or at least sparked

Tibetan house demon.

off by spirits and demons. They are the creatures who in pictorial art are often depicted as men with animal attributes like wings, horns, and buck feet having in Europe since some hundred years emigrated mostly from our mental sphere (16) surviving, however, unchanged, in non-industrialized civilisations where they cause evil. The events of life, this being the decisive point, are not considered blind accidents there, but regarded as the acts of personified powers each bearing its own name. This magic explanatory pattern which has become strange to us moves back into our sphere of comprehension if one refrains from understanding demons and spirits to be living beings which whisper in the trees at night and are hence at home outside the human person. But if you follow the idea of demons being psychic powers negatively or positively loaded and settled within man himself the whole matter acquires a different and more acceptable aspect: the difference between the old belief in ghosts and modern psychiatry tends to shrink by and large.

Let us sum up: luck, this being the first thesis, is neither favour nor accident. It can rather be achieved even if this notion of the manageability of luck is not in harmony really with the conventional occidental norms. Our somewhat antiquated definition of luck can be replaced by an at least quite practical idea or supplemented by such, namely that luck is the absence of misfortune. The second thesis ensues from the first: provided luck is no accidental product but an achievable one then misfortune can likewise be no accident; it is a phenomenon for which the person concerned is responsible. So misfortune presents itself as a self-inflicted illness which implies the extension of the definition of illness to calamity. Consequently the achievement of luck must be understood as a healing process in the course of which the unlucky or unhappy person is recovering in the direction of luck or happiness, the healing process itself appearing as a form of banning evil demons. This brings us to the question of how luck is to be managed. In principle the answer

Red tiger demon.

is simple. What one needs is a ritual and for it a dagger furnished with the special faculty to expell interfering, dangerous or illness bringing demons if not sending them to glory. I avoid, you will probably notice, quite deliberately the word 'to kill'. The demons are - it is said officially - not killed because they too belong to the 'sentient beings' which a believing Buddhist must not kill. The key-word in this context is 'banning' or 'liberating'. By such ban one should, however, not imagine a rather delicate and distinguished matter. In the life story of Nagarjuna, a renowned Buddhist saint, we for example find this episod:

While studying at the Nalanda monastery Nagarjuna once felt irritated by the presence of a young girl who, it is said, was waiting upon the monks there. What her services implied is not reported. Nagarjuna now by virtue of his refined perception recognizes: this woman was not

Meteoric Iron Yes or No?

born by man but it is the incarnation of a demon goddess named Candika. In order to bring back to the path of purity his own and his bretheren's thoughts, Nagarjuna locks up the demonic girl in the monastery kitchen by driving a Phurpa into the ground of the monastery yard (in front of the kitchen door): the dagger is now barring her, the disguised demon's, exit. Thereupon she approaches the cook promising to oblige him carnally if only he would pull out of the ground and burn the dagger placed in front of the kitchen door. The cook succumbs to the temptation. The she-demon thus found out turns tail. The monks of the Nalanda monastery may resume their meditation exercises without interference by unchaste thoughts.

This somewhat drastic story leads to the question what specifications daggers must correspond to so that they can ban demons. The dagger Nagarjuna drove into the ground of the monastery court was obviously made of wood. Because how else could the cook have burnt it in the kitchen range? And indeed: to this day one may find in bazaars and Tibetan markets wooden daggers in great number. That is one side. On the other side one can hear and read that the really banning dagger which is capable of overpowering the demons must be made

དཔལ་མགོན་ཀླུ་སྒྲུབ

Nagarjuna

of iron, better still of meteoric iron (18). I personally have only seen iron daggers in the active ritual practice and have got the impression that wooden daggers were serving more passive purposes, e.g. for marking a site which is to be protected against demons. Below I shall stick to the iron version.

Old Phurpas with bronze hilts.

Now, are these iron Phurpas really made of meteoric iron, of 'celestial iron' as is prescribed in the rules and stressed time and again by the dagger men? Because I wanted to make sure I once packed six old iron Phurpas into a brief-case and took them for inspection to some metallurgists who were going to submit them to a spectral analysis in the laboratory of a steel plant. The procedure is the ignition on the surface of the iron, e.g. the dagger blade, of an electric spark. Its light is then dispersed and analysed by an expensive apparatus which already

SPECTRAL ANALYSIS

of six all-iron Phurpas, Thyssen Edelstahlwerke, Witten (FRG), 27 Nov. 1984:

	Dagger no. 9	Dagger no. 13	Dagger no. 11	Dagger no. 14	Dagger no. 6	Dagger no. 10
Weight (g)	330	625	198	193	305	340
Length (cm)	28.7	24.6	21.2	21.9	23.5	25.5
ANALYSIS OF CONTENTS (per cent)						
Carbon	0.340	1.500	1.400	0.570	1.000	1.200
Manganese	0.020	0.020	0.020	0.020	0.390	0.034
Molybdenite	0.078	0.040	0.046	0.040	0.040	0.071
Vanadium	0.011	0.010	0.010	0.010	0.010	0.010
Aluminium	0.019	0.029	0.017	0.020	0.061	0.036
Silicon	0.088	0.270	0.140	0.085	0.340	0.230
Chromium	0.020	0.020	0.020	0.020	0.020	0.020
Nickel	0.086	0.069	0.030	0.030	0.030	0.030
Tungsten	0.020	0.020	0.020	0.020	0.020	0.020
Lead	0.050	0.050	0.050	0.050	0.050	0.050
Iron	99.000	98.000	98.000	99.000	98.000	98.000

after a few seconds spits out a strip of paper. On it one can read which other metals may have been amalgamated with the iron. The rule now is that meteoric iron must contain a minimum of five percent nickel. You can see the result of the analysis on the table: in all the six daggers we find minimal traces of nickel yet none of the daggers at least approximately attains the five percent minimum of nickel which would allow to assume the iron to be ot meteoric origin (19).

Is the contention that Phurpas consist of meteoric iron herewith reduced to a legend of the type one so ofter comes across in the field of the dagger cult? Yes and no. One cannot exclude for instance that Tibetan iron foundries have added minimal quantities of meteorite iron to the molten material perhaps by scraping off a few chippings from a lump of of nickel-iron that has come down somewhere. In so doing the ritual instruction would have been observed. It is, however, impossible to clarify this issue any more: Today the daggers are only here and there forged manually from imported iron rods. The majority originates from Indian foundries and there they are cast without any particular ceremony.

And what do the dagger men say to all this? On one hand they insist on the meteor theory. Yet themselves they judge the quality of daggers by quite different criteria e.g. by their sound: they snap with a fingernail against the blade and test if the dagger produces a long and well audible sound. This happens with few daggers only. And they also appreciate very much if a Phurpa has a magic 'pedigree', i.e. if it has been for generations in the possession of recognized dagger lamas having thus sort of accumulated banning powers. Other characteristics such as hammered magic formulae (mantras) and other decorative details seem of less importance to them (20).

The Iconography of Daggers

Especially American tibetologists have made just these aesthetic aspects the object of their studies. However, only partially satisfying results have been obtained. One of these results is the finding that Phurpas cannot be properly classified. Each dagger has its own individuality. One does not really resemble the other and even family likenesses meaning the recognizable origin from the same workshop can but rarely be ascertained. In the following daggers can, therefore, only with great caution be described generally.

As one may see on the pictures in this book there is still some sort of ideal type of a Phurpa. Describing it by beginning from the bottom, it stands in a socket shaped as an equilateral triangle reminding the beholder of that triangular stone box in which Padmasambhava is said to have found the ritual scriptures on the dagger cult. The dagger handler can remove the Phurpa from the socket as well as replace it again. Then comes the three-edged iron blade, the length of which is often ornamented with meandering snakes. And the blade in turn sticks in the mouth of a makara. This is the Sanskrit

word for 'crocodile'. What is meant here, however, is a mythical monster existing merely in our imagination not yet discovered by biologists. Above the makara head there is generally an 'eternal knot'. This is a symbol of luck otherwise known by the name of 'Buddha's intestines'.

The handle consists either of a stylized lotus blossom. This applies for the more peaceful daggers, or it consists of an often five-pointed thunderbolt applying to the Phurpas of a more threatening nature. After another eternal knot comes Phurpa's three-faced head, often but not always baring his teeth in wrath (21). The upper end is occasionally shaped like a horse's head reminding one of Tamdin, the horse god, or some other Buddhist symbol such as perhaps a half-dorje, a 'wishfulfilling jewel' or a 'dabla', the personal deity of the original owner. But all these features may be lacking. What is decisive is just the iron and the three-edged blade. And what do the silk kerchiefs, sometimes tied to the dagger's hilt, stand for? Some dagger men say the piece of silk cloth is serving merely as upholstery to prevent the dagger from rattling in its copper or brass container. Others declare that the cloth is supposed to hide the dagger from the looks of inquisitive characters (men and demons). Yet others maintain the silk flag which is frequently only a black or blue-black rag is meant to stabilize the Phurpa on its trajectory when the dagger practitioner hurls it against a demon (22). Finally the cloth serves, so it is said, as 'the god's garment'.

The God-Dagger

A ritual dagger is, therefore, no dead instrument, no mere knife, but a deity as well. And I stress: as well, at the same time. Phurpas are simultaneously lifeless instruments, ritual implements as well as a living deity that is likewise called Phurpa. In other words: whenever a person takes such a dagger into his hand he grips the Phurpa deity with his fingers: deity and knife are one and there is no space in between the two of even a hair. Such an equation is not exactly common to an occidental. Of course we too have images of God, the crucifix and statues of the Holy Virgin. But these images, and this is the difference, only symbolize the deity; they serve as emblems. With the Phurpa it is different: The dagger is a divine being.

This unity of dagger and god confronts even the Phurpa followers with sometimes peculiar problems such as: what is one to do with a ritual dagger no longer in use because its possessor had died without having appointed a (spiritual) heir? The Tibet writer Alexandra David-Neel (23) reports such a case: she comes upon a group of frightened peasants carrying with them a dagger of their recently deceased lama in a chest intending to stow it away secretly - namely on the territory of a neighbouring village - in a cave. Their own land they disliked to infect with the incalculable dagger powers. In consequence of these magical disposal problems some daggers have attained venerable age. Their handles are worn and

‹ Iron Phurpa coated with brass and sacrificial bowl.

polished by centuries of swearing, praying, and rolling between the palms: once they are forged and consecrated one cannot easily get rid of them again.

And who is Phurpa? This question cannot be answered to the last detail. Deities of the Himalayas can mostly not be conceived as clearly definable individuals. More often than not they are emanations or personifications of other deities and it remains at times uncertain who personifies whom. It is, however, undisputed that Phurpa stands in relationship with the horse god Tamdin whose Sanskrit name is Hayagriva which amounts to 'the one with the horse's head'. Here again we find a relation to the nomads, to the consecration of the soil, and to the tent pegs. Over and above that Phurpa is also regarded as a belligerent emanation of a principle which is manifest in the deities Mahakala, (a distant relative of the Indian Shiva), in Avalokiteshvara, the patron of Tibet, and last but not least in 'Guru Rinpoche', in Padmasambhava that Indian sage who allegedly had discovered and perfected the dagger cult (24).

Despite its pre-buddhist origin Phurpa, by which is now meant the deity aspect, is by no means counted among the lower deities. On the contrary: the monks of the Sakya order, one of the Tibetan sects, worship Mahakala-Phurpa as their patron to whom every monk has to pray every day with the dagger between his palms. Above that Phurpa yet enjoys another function in the Buddhist pantheon: since his, if only partly successful, incorporation into Tibetan Buddhism the wrathful horse god serves as the 'protector of the doctrine' i.e. as defender of Buddhism against its human and demoniacal enemies.

The Phurpa, still under his deity aspect, deserves an appropriate veneration, too. A planet, Jupiter, is assigned to him as well as a day of the week: Thursday is dedicated to him (25). His followers celebrate a yearly Phurpa feast which as a rule is in the month of August (26). On this occasion the monks scatter an artful mandala, a world diagram, with coloured sand on the temple floor the way you can see it on the photograph: in the centre of the mandala (27) stands a big Phurpa which might be around 60 cm high surrounded by wooden guardian daggers clad in red jackets. When you look closely you can possibly recognize in the upper left corner of the picture a monk rolling a ritual dagger between his palms.

You should remember this picture in case you should ever be tempted to buy a Phurpa yourself. In the course of the preceding rambling of antique shops, bazaars, and auctioners one comes, occasionally, across daggers of the most varying types: either they are made of wood and, therefore, not corresponding to the ritual instruction (prescribing iron for expulsion daggers); or they are so big that they could not be rolled between the palms. The solution of the miracle is that in the dagger world there are at least three main categories of Phurpas: daggers only used for worship (the central Phurpa of the mandala),

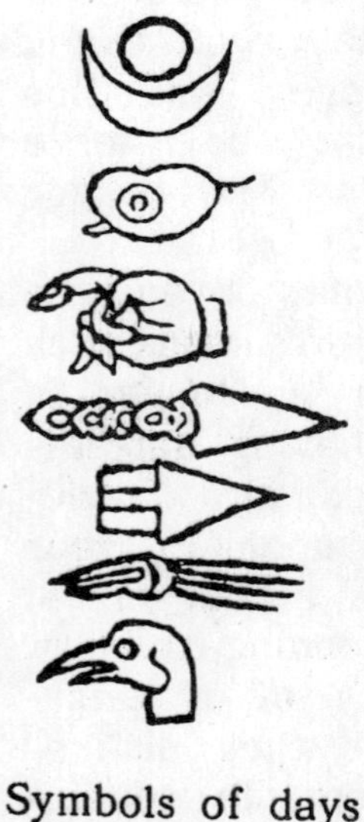

Symbols of days of the week.

wooden daggers for passive or defensive magic (guarding the mandala on the picture), and, thirdly, the proper 'diamond princes': iron daggers which are rolled between the palms of one's hands for exorcism rituals (28).

How Old are Ritual Daggers?

The seller of a Phurpa will probably assure you it is an ancient piece dating from the 13th or 14th century. You will then have another sip of your tea and ask your business partner how he could possibly know that? In fact the age of a dagger can hardly be ascertained for sure. The actually proper method, the 14-C-procedure (29), is out of question when it comes to determining the age of a dagger: the carbon content in the dagger iron amounts to less than one percent. Consequently one would have to sacrifice an entire dagger for the test. So the prospective buyer usually has no other choice than to put up with the (often enough though not always correct) assumption that a much used dagger must also be an old one. The traces of use can partly be seen and partly felt when one rolls the Phurpa between one's hands for a try.

What kind of people are they who use the magic dagger and practice the Phurpa cult? One ought to be wary of generalisations in this respect. But one gets the impression they are mostly elderly people not necessarily coming from the upper strata of society. Comparable to the nonmedical practitioners in the west they have, on the basis of a special gift and often after years of endeavour, found their way to the Phurpa cult. The dagger adepts - should one speak of spiritual self-made men? - moreover do not belong to the Gelugpa order (30). That is the order of the 'yellow caps' who since about the year 1650 have directed the spiritual and the profane life in Tibet and from whose midst the respective Dalai Lama originates, including His Holiness the present 14. Dalai Lama. The dagger men rather belong to those sects which since the turn of the 14th century have been pushed into a socio-political background.

Phurpa Practitioners

These monks or lamas, however, do not always correspond to the western ideas of a clergyman: many, not all, are married. Some, not all of them, wear a monk's robe. The dividing line between a priest and a spiritually advanced layman cannot be exactly drawn. They are apparently all males. During my wanderings through the dagger world I rarely found anything pointing to females who had been initiated into the Phurpa cult (31). The monastic consecration does not do any harm but it constitutes no condition. Likewise the Phurpa practitioner need not observe any ascetic rules such as sexual abstinence or a vegetarian diet (32).

The meeting with dagger men, real magicians or conjurers, never takes an uneasy or sinister course. They are mostly people of pleasant self-assuredness, humourous liveliness and cordial calmness with whom one usually gets into conversation easily inspite of the cultural distance, provided that the yellow-haired stranger succeeds in wiping the already mentioned problem off the table, namely the question why anyone should be interested in the dagger cult without desiring to exercise it. I might perhaps add that the question of money has never played a decisive role in these meetings. Of course the man of world will, in accordance with Asian habits, always leave an appropriate gift in cash behind: magicians, too, must eat. Confidence, and that is what matters, can better be achieved by other kinds of presents. In this connexion it does not do any harm to be able to sing a German or French song to them or to show the lady of the house how one kisses a lady's hand strictly by Prussian rule: Tibetans, including magicians, like a good lough.

Despite their often varying origin, education, and sect affiliation the dagger people have invariably one thing in common: their profound training in the tantra

Scorpion charm against evil demons.

doctrine (33). The older ones among them have in many cases graduated from the tantric faculty of a monastic university in Tibet. Others might have undergone a less formal tantric training (34). Anyhow, tantra is the theory without which no dagger practitioner can do. What is tantra? The Sanskrit dictionary enumerates not less than ten different meanings of the word (35). There are, however two main meanings: firstly tantra stands for weaving, texture, or weaving mill. Secondly the word signifies books of magic contents.

What is Tantra?

Running the risk of being scolded by learned tantrics I venture to say two things: number one, I will present only those constituents of the tantra doctrine which are indispensable for the comprehension of the Phurpa cult thereby omitting quite important other elements. Number two, I take the liberty of wiping its oriental disconcerting coloration off the separated elements which only too easily

Phurpa Practitioner demonstrating a mudra.

embarrasses the western observer. In this reduced form the tantric doctrine firstly appears as a language whose aggregation of symbols has partly been laid down in books. This language is, however, not suitable for human communication. It is an occult language - nothing comparable is known to us - which might bear a resemblance to programming languages like Basic or Cobol whithout the command of which we could no longer set anything really in motion these days.

Occult Language

Like these computer languages the tantric occult language consists of a number of orders called 'mantras' (36) which of course do not serve the dialogue between man and machine but the conversation with the timeless world and its inhabiltants, no matter if they be demons or psychic powers within man himself. This makes it obvious why dagger handlers cannot do without a tantric training: it is their very task to communicate with the forces controlling luck and misfortune. And in doing so they use that magic programming language, the mantras. Mantras in turn are words mainly derived from Sanskrit, an old Indian liturgic language, similar to church Latin. The immediate literal sense of the mantras is sometimes unambiguous and distinct. The Phurpa e.g. is in Sanskrit 'kila' or 'kilaya'. It has found its entrance into mantrism as 'kila'. Another part of the mantra vocabulary consists of words without any definite meaning but expressing emotional qualities. One of these is the mantra OM which is supposed to evoke something like a sensation of entirety, or PHAT signalling 'release yourself'. The third and by far the biggest part of mantras, though, is void of sense and does not mean anything that could be closely defined.

Now, what is the good of a language largely consisting of void words? This leads us to a second version of tantrism: although tantra is in the first place a language or a vocabulary, the use of these words is based on a particular vibration theory of which the first dogma says: acoustic signals like carefully articulated syllables or series of syllables, such as the famous Tibetan mantra OM MANI PADME HUM, produce pictures or optical sensation. The acoustic waves create, no, are simultaneously light waves. This sounds rather odd. And yet even to occidentals this multi-dimensional form of perception is basically familiar. The quality of music or poetry we partly appreciate according to the acoustic signal sequences creating pictures in our mind or not. And vice versa visual sensations such as contemplating a work of art produce in the expert beholder an acoustic echo, a sound effect. A painting 'tells' you something. Or it tells you nothing.

This relationship of a reflected image of sound and light which in our part of the world is restricted to the fringe of experience is in the tantric doctrine the starting point of a fully developed theory of refined perception. The articulation of a certain sound wave structure, possibly the mantra OM AH HUM or PHAT, not merely produces a faded or coincidental picture but a determinable piece

Phurpa practitioner.

of visual reality which for the trained tantric is not less real than the reality of a lower order that can be photographed and with which the layman must normally be satisfied. The mantras here function as fuses setting certain perceptive processes in motion and setting fields of experience free for the dagger man which commonly remain closed and inaccessible.

And what sort of fields of experience are they? At this stage I ought to point out first that people who have grown up in Asia, no matter whether they have undergone tantric training or not, perceive more or better than a European anyway. This refined perceptive power, an otherwise not explicable cultural distinction, may be considerably enhanced by systematic training. One can e.g. endeavour to observe people or objects sharply or with less focussed eyes, that is like silhouettes. Or one attempts, this being another example, to dissect the visual everyday reality into minimal perceptive fields, hence to see the world as if through a powerful magnifying glass. Or one practises not to see the actual objects but the spaces in between the peculiar shapes which usually escape the observer. Furthermore one can finish with the habitual selective vision, at least for ten minutes, and consequently discover visual riches which the untrained eye mostly does not perceive. The result of such exercises is an impression .as if somebody had wiped your windscreen so to speak.

Smelling with the Finger Tips

So much for the mere sight. But man disposes of five senses or even six if you count as a sense the sensation of space and time. These sense channels, mainly experienced separately, a trained tantric - this being the next step - can tie up to a network of all-embracing perception in a fabulous fashion. Light waves and sound waves, sense of smell and hearing are interwoven into one entity like warp and woof. The aim of tantric training after all is man smelling with his finger tip, hearing with his eyes, being able to see with his ears and thus achieving total perception. What appears to normal man as an unchangeable world is transformed into sensual material that can be shaped, into a sort of theatre on whose scene the schooled dagger practitioner may himself produce the figures and the plot calling them up by his mantras.

After the theory there is now a bit of dagger practice. How does one ignite realities? As an example may serve a little ritual comparable to an early morning devotion, a 'Lord's Prayer', the way it ought to be the daily routine of any dagger practitioner. The purpose of the ritual is to protect all sentient beings, hence also you and me, from evil. This evil, called Mara (37), is, unlike the way we see it in our imagination, not aggressiveness. Mara is the ignorance from which emanate death, disease and and love.This daily Mara exorcism begins quite plainlywith a lonely man sitting early in the morning hidden somewhere in the vast Himalayas with a butter lamp in
37 front of him, a photo of his guru and an image of his

yidam, his personal patron deity. The dagger stands before him in a triangular socket made of unbaked clay. He then seizes the Phurpa and puts it between his palms. The dagger will now roll between his hands, a couple of seconds above his head, then in front of his mouth, finally before his chest. Along with this the dagger man recites in a slightly declining and moaning scale a chain of syllables possibly running as follows:

OM RULU RULU HUM SHOA HUM
OM BHASER KILI KILAYA SARVAR
BING NE BAM HUM PHET.

The meaning of these signal words floats in the twilight zone between comprehensibility and linguistic darkness. With some imagination one could derive from this chain of syllables that there is mention of a great and sacred matter (OM), that a polymorphous being (SARVAR) is scolded earnestly (HUM) and threatened with a Phurpa (KILA, KILAYA) and that he, the polymorphous, ought to disappear (PHET). The remaining mantras are either ambiguous or incomprehensible considering that, owing to phonetic variations of dialect, their meaning might be influenced too (38). This syllable chain the dagger man will repeat not less than a hundred and eight times and with each repetition the picture of the world threatened by Mara becomes more intense. And this not merely in the sense of an imagination nor in the fashion of a hallucination at all, instead as the result of an improved perceptive faculty achieved through exercises. For this process not easily understandable for us there is a foreign word: he 'ideates' Mara and the the world he infests. The word is derived from Greek 'idea', the original look, or also from 'eidolon', the picture.

A Fight Against Mara

And what does an ideated reality look like? One does not hear anything precise on that. But one gets the impression that a world contemplated by a dagger practitioner must well differ from the sphere-shaped earth as photographed from the moon by astronauts. It is more of a disc floating in the ocean the centre of which is Mount Kailash. This is a Himalayan peak in the border region of India, Nepal and Tibet in the vicinity of which four great rivers have their source: Brahmaputra, Ganges, Indus and Yamuna. On the western edge of the disc - America not yet being discovered - live the Feringhi, the "Franks", the Europeans, you and I, and today the Americans certainly included. Mara, the evil, not necessarily appears as a demon with horns and claws. The polymorphous is able to make his appearance in the most varied diguises, be it in the form of a cloud perhaps, which the dagger handler threatens with his Phurpa, cuts up and drives away.

After roughly an hour which is the time needed for the recital of the syllabic chain the dagger practitioner will let the picture fade away. Meanwhile there is daylight. The peaks have taken on a yellow colouring. The valley is full of fog and the Feringhi looking on may wonder if such rituals could induce anything? The answer is preponderantly yes. I personally am not entirely unmoved by the thought that somewhere in the orient there sit men with daggers in their hands fighting against evil also

Demons of Mara in Gandhara sculptures (Lahore Museum).

for my sake while I am on the icy Gotthard motorway late at night. Is this consciousness in itself not a sufficient effect?

Yet appealing to a person's devotional feelings would not be appropriate to the matter. Actually the dagger people handle their ignition words and realities in a fascinatingly mechanistic fashion. They regard this production of realities as a perfectly normal thing, the same as we do not really feel any surprise when our car starts and begins to move upon turning the ignition key. The world, this being a general understanding, does not really exist. We form it in our minds. Maybe I should add another example for that: I remember a conversation with a dagger man on the issue of how best to make a yantra (39). These are simple geometrical figures, mainly equilateral triangles, which one must draw on the ground in front of oneself for exorcism ceremonies. How are such yantras done? By scratching the ground? With dying powder? By markings with guardian daggers? The reply obtained ran equivalent to this: 'You may do this in one way or another. But why don't you just make the yantra in your head?'.

Ritual Gestures

The learning of mantras of which there are theoretically thousands does, however, not complete the training in tantrism. A good tantric and dagger handler must be attentive not only with his soul and language but also include his body. This inclusion is achieved by way of a body or manual lingo: the dagger man supplements the acoustic mantra sequences by visual sign sequences resembling the finger language sport divers use for communication under water or those hand signals employed by the deaf-mute for conversation among each other. These ritual gestures, called 'mudras' (40), fulfill similar functions as the mantras: those of a sign language for communication with the other world. They are also of ancient Indian origin differing, however, from the mantras in some respects. On the one hand their reservoir of signs is relatively limited: there are hardly more than a hundred mudras really in use. As opposed to the mantras, which form a twilight-language, the mudras are preponderantly not obscure signals. Their meaning is largely clear. Here are some examples: The first mudra (to be performed together with a dorje-thunderbolt) stands for 'protection'. Then follows the mudra for 'invocation'. The third sign with the spread out index finger and the little finger signals 'defence'. It is often used in the dagger cult and is roughly identical in meaning with the mantra PHAT, which is pronounced PHET in Tibetan. Now comes the hand-sign for 'union' or 'communion'. And here (overleaf) finally is the perfectly classical dagger mudra that sets the stream of spititual energy in motion against Mara, the polymorphous one: the rolling of the dagger between the palms of one's hands (40).

I again sum up: there are three main types of ritual dagger. Only the medium sized Phurpas which can be effortlessly rolled between the palms are suitable for exorcism ceremonies. These daggers that can be used in exorcism are made totally or partly of iron. This dagger iron contains traces of nickel. It is, however, contrary to the constant hearsay, no meteoric iron. The iron daggers are simultaneously instrument and deity for which reason one may not simply throw Phurpas away. The dagger practitioners mostly belong to the Nyingmapa sect, or

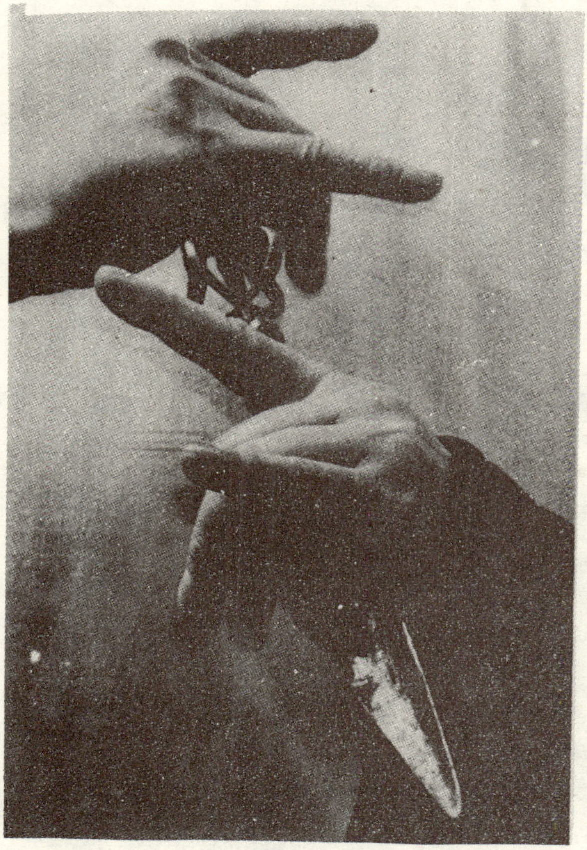

'Protection'

'Invocation'

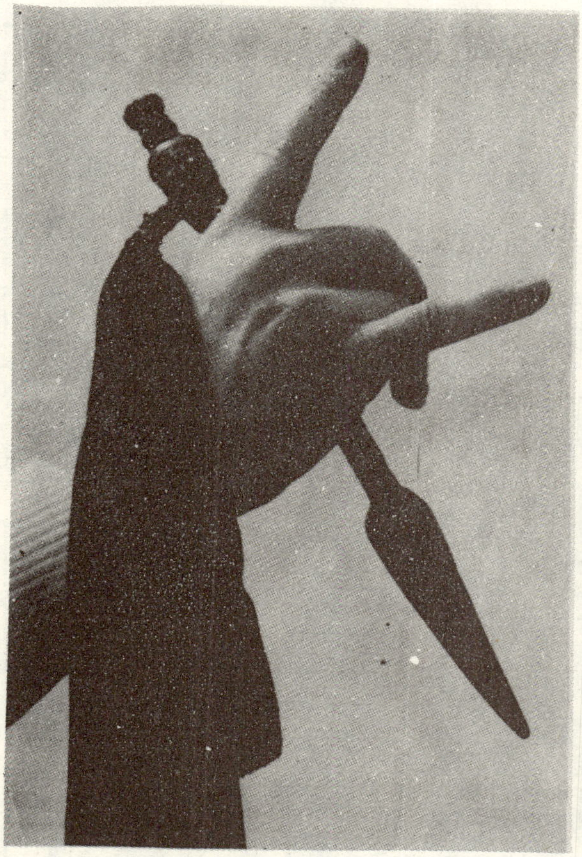

'Defence'

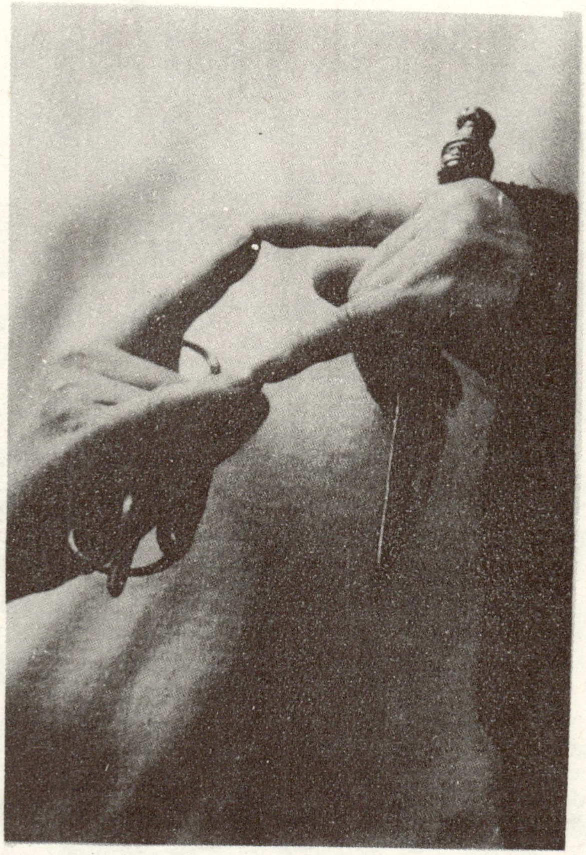

Communion'

Starting the energy stream against Mara by rolling the Phurpa between the the palms.

the order of the red caps. They are all trained in tantrism. Tantra is - besides many other things - the doctrine of the magic spells (mantras) and gestures (mudras) by the aid of which reality dimensions, magic battle-fields can be produced where the actual fight against the evil-bringing forces takes place.

The Dark Side of the Phurpa Cult

Up to this point the Phurpa cult presents itself as a respectable piece of ancient world wisdom, adorned with the venerableness of a long history and a rich and strong culture. Attached to this is a quite pretentious theory which demands great efforts from one's power of imagination and flexibility of mind. Yet this beautiful semblance is misleading: the dagger cult has its dark side, too. It has always been up to our present day the horror of all orthodox Buddhists. One may even say: in the spiritually determined Tibetan culture the ritual daggers tend to play the role which in our science-oriented world is attributed to chemical weapons.

This many-sided problem (42) can here be only briefly outlined: he who is mastering the dagger cult, the method of making happy, is naturally also gifted with the capacity of causing misfortune. He is able to direct the hailstorm to his enemy's fields. He can by his own discretion or by instruction of his client kill people from the distance. He is capable of contaminating entire regions with demons. The dagger power is the creeping danger of which nobody may feel safe. This fear of the dagger men abusing their knowledge by causing misfortune instead of only luck has even found its way into the liturgy of Vajrayana Buddhism. In a recital in honour of the deity Tara which is roughly the Tibetan virgin Mary one may e. g. find the following lines (43):

> There the many beautiful treasures,
> the food of nine flavours, of ten sweetnesses,
> the retinue of servants, the thirty little men,
> the medicine, the incense, the bright lamps
> we give to you in offering!
>
> Accept this with a willing mind
> but avert, turn back the strength
> of the magicians (against themselves)
> who roll the magic dagger between their palms,
> who fling white mustard seed as magic,
> who cast their magic weapons...

If one hears this pleading prayer, one may ask why the monks should be afraid of the dagger handlers since they, those clad in red, usually have themselves a Phurpa standing in their temple and know how to use it, too. Is this not a contradiction in itself? This question may only be very carefully answered: as so many other people also Buddhists, laymen as well as monks, have two 'souls' in their chest, namely an orthodox one that must reject the Phurpa cult (44) and a pre-Buddhist one which may not subscribe to the dagger cult yet pays the old pagan Phurpa power tribute after all and recognizes it.

The Little Bird the Dogs Vainly Try to Snap at

Let me explain this in a few words. No life philosophy, no view of the world, no theory is entirely void of any contradiction. The dagger cult in Vajrayana Buddhism, however, is more painful than just a small contradiction: the dagger cult indicates a rift that runs right through the history of Buddhism. The Phurpa cult is the salient

༄།།སྒྲོལ་མ་ལྗངས་ཁུ།།

The Green Tara.

point, the worm which does not die. In one of the sacred texts attached to this book it says that the dagger cult is 'the little bird the dogs vainly try to snap at'. And where does this rift run? The monasteries and the monks are known to depend largely on the donations and fees provided by the believers, on the copper coins and gifts of the herdsmen and peasants. These rather simple people have never really managed to find their way with the pure Buddhist teaching. In the first place Gautama Buddha's speeches were hardly known to them, the 'donating masters'. The dogma of the eightfold path was not even taught to the people. The pulpit function of the clergy, so distinct in Christianity and Islam, one would seek in traditional Vajrayana Buddhism in vain.

The householders and donating masters also continued to live with their traditional demon and dagger beliefs because the pure form of Buddhism - and this probably applies to all highly developed religions - does not offer very much to unlearned people: a finely spun ethic postponing salvation to a life after death, demanding renunciation and even a painful change of personality, attempting to deny the people just what they love to have: sex and a gulp from the liquor bottle. Opposed to that is the old sensual magic with its pomp and power which so far

Telephone : 685

བོད་གཞུང་ཆོས་རིག་ལས་ཁུངས།

COUNCIL FOR RELIGIOUS AND CULTURAL AFFAIRS
OF H. H, THE DALAI LAMA

Gangchen Kyishong,
Dharamsala-176215
Distt. Kangra
Himachal Pradesh.

March 1, 1986

Dear Mr. Marcotty,

thank you for your letter of February 8th, 1986. I apologize for my inability to write you sooner because of other commitments outside of Dharamsala.

In your letter dated October 12, 1985 to the Private Office of His Holiness, you have asked two questions regarding the Phurpa practice. I will respond as follows:

1. Phurpa is a Nyingmapa deity and its practice is in accordance with Buddhism. Your publication will not harm the reputation of Buddhism.

2. In Tantric practices, the practitioner, motivated by compassion, destroys hostile demons to prevent them from accumulating additional sins by harming other beings. Therefore, the Phurpa practice does not violate any Buddhist doctrine.

I hope you will find this information useful. Should you have any other specific questions on the subject, please let us know.

With best wishes,

Yours Sincerely

Kalsang Yeshi
General Secretary
Council for religious and cultural affairs.

KY/tc

prohibits nothing but instead recommends refined and ritualised forms of lust and ecstasy. There is the dagger cult promising happiness here and now and not at some later date after a series of alleged and in any case hardly predictable reincarnations. Are our whereabouts after death really that important?

The Dogmatic Problem

In this fashion over the centuries emerged what we would call a material duress: the Buddhist clergy dependant upon the taxes and donations received from the laymen had to adapt itself, give in to the pressure of the dagger believers and desert substantial dogmatic bastions. One example for this may suffice: according to Buddha's teaching killing, or 'robbing of life', counts among the very severe sins which throw man back very far on his way to the nirvana. That is one side of the matter. On the other side it cannot be concealed that the killing of a demon represents the climax of the traditional Phurpa cult the way it is described in the sacred texts attached to this book. And the demons are regarded as sentient beings which one must not kill. This makes the contradiction obvious: An orthodox Buddhist cannot consent to the dagger cult if he wants to remain faithful to the letter of the doctrine.

But also with the spirit of Buddhism the dagger cult is hardly in harmony. In the old ritual texts there are instructions how the dagger practitioner has to kill not only the body but also the soul of the enemy demon meaning: the defeated demon is not merely robbed of his life but of his chance of reincarnation, too (45). Is it in consequence hopelessly excluded from the circle of death and rebirth? One may also read the dagger man ought to pounce upon the vigour of the demons 'with a wolf's greed', gulping it down or sucking it up in order to prolong his own life by it. 'You dream', we can read, 'of killing sentient beings, of madness, of sharp axes and trees crashing down. You dream of killing the Ging female demons. You cook them. You feed on their life-substance'. Believing Buddhists must not follow such instructions.

In theory, therefore, the front is clearly marked: anybody may decide in favour or against the dagger cult. This should clarify the situation. But that is just theory. In practice nobody knows who has the magic dagger hidden in his belt. Who sees what happens at night on the cemeteries? One devines this and whispers that about who is handling the black-poisenous dagger cult of the left hand: why should a woman have died here in childbed? Or why has the cattle of a neighbouring village died of foot-and-mouth disease? Are the dagger men behind it? The dagger cult has poisened the atmosphere also because everybody joined in: the Bön people who are the followers of the non-Buddhist forms of cult still active also in these days. The red-caps anyway. And even some Gelugpa, the reformed yellow-caps, secretly roll the dagger between their palms. But one also cannot trust the laymen, the hermits, and the roaming beggars either. Who knows who

Head of an old Phurpa with crown showing the five Tathagatas.

of them adores the dagger and throws the white mustard seed clandestinely?

The Rules of Peaceful Coexistence

The dispute about the dagger cult (and other tantric practices) does not seperate recognizable sects or groups from one another. The rift rather runs between the black and the white half of the heart of anyone concerned. This cleft has never been glued over the centuries. However, the representatives of Buddhist orthodoxy, the dignitaries at Lhasa, and the dagger adepts have learnt apparently how to get on with eachother. There must have been negotiations between them with the aim of avoiding the misuse of the Phurpa and to open the road to a peaceful coexistence of followers and opponents of the dagger doctrine. The dagger men are at least now willing to submit to a voluntary self-control of which the most important rules are (46):

- Phurpa rituals must not begin without prior invocation of Lord Buddha nor end without such. This was not always a matter of course.
- The dagger man must never use the dagger to his own advantage be it to enrich himself or to make people subservient to himself.
- If the Phurpa practitioner does use the dagger in his own favour all the same he must be able to give ten valid and honourable reasons.
- He is always permitted to use his weapon to help other people or in defense of Tibet and Tibetan Buddhism against their enemies.
- The dagger pratitioner is forbidden to cause more than necessary harm. He may for example not 'completely' devastate a place by his Phurpa power.
- When performing the ritual the practitioner must be in a state of complete peace of mind: He must have subdued bad emotions like hatred or lust of murder.

The opponents to the dagger cult, among these above all the members of the yellow cap order, have in turn made a few steps to meet the dagger adepts halfway. Since a historically not precisely fixed date (until the Chinese occupation) a ceremonial procession from the Sera monastery to the Potala, the seat of the Dalai Lama, used to take place every year. The pontiff of the yellow church then used to bless by touching it a Phurpa otherwise kept in the Sera monastery. This dagger is according to a legend said to have flown in ancient times from India across the Himalayas and have fallen down on the monasteries premises (47).

And what is the position today? All concerned endeavour to reduce the old antagonism as much as possible. When you ask the rinpoches, the dignitaries of Vajrayana-Buddhism, how the dagger cult could be reconciled with the teachings of Gautama Buddha you get various answers. Some say Gautama himself had taught the dagger cult, 'the wheel of the sharp weapons', but hidden the texts away until man will have become mature for the Phurpa Dharma. Therefore, one could not very well speak of an antagonism. Others mean the old sacred texts should not be taken word by word but like so many things in tantrism symbolically. One is not permitted, so they object, to talk about 'killing' the evil bringing demons or human beings. What happens is that the dagger practitioner 'liberates' them, the evil spirits, from their inferior existence helping them to a higher existence in a Buddha land (48).

But up to this day there remains a residue: the suspicion, the fear of the power of the magicians throwing the mustard seed and letting their power weapons crash down. The Tibetan government in exile now residing in Dharamsala to the north of the Indian capital Delhi rests reserved. On the one hand they have advised their missionary monks in Europe and the United States not to put the dagger cult (and also other tantric practices) into the forefront of their instruction if possible. On the other hand the presently reigning 14th Dalai Lama has never denounced the Phurpa cult. In his entourage there is even a proper dagger priest and hail master (49) whose duty it is to provide for fine weather for big events in the open.

Phurpa Life Style

Before I turn to the actual exorcism let me mention that the dagger experts do not exclusively use their Phurpas in the framework of solemn cults only. The daggers are for all intents and purposes part of daily routine and produced and unwrapped for all sorts of events. Firstly for the object-bound meditation which I will later deal with in more detail. And then for dancing (50), especially in the course of the masked dances, so popular in the Himalayas, which are meant to demonstrate to the spectators the victory of Buddhism over the old sorcerers and animists. In the past the Phurpa was also used as a weapon in defense of the wild yak (51). Next the Phurpa was in use for speed-walking. By this we must understand leaping in long jumps on uneven or stony ground. This was done for the purpose of shortening long times of walking. The speed-walker as is reported (52) thereby holds the Phurpa with the fingers of his right hand by the upper end, the blade pointing vertically down. The adept puts himself into a state of mind similar to trance and bounds forward in long leaps. Meanwhile the dagger is holding the ground spirits at bay and assures that the speed-walker will always tread on the ground safely even over long distances without stumbling or falling.

In addition to these now rather rare or possibly extinct uses, yak banning and speed-walking, there is weather making, still practiced at present, which is principally to be understood as the defense from hailstorms, which in a region of highly variable climate like the Himalayas are particularly dreaded. The duty of the hail-master is to encircle endangered areas with (wooden) guardian daggers, thus marking them and to avert oncoming thunderclouds with his Phurpa (53). The weather makers were in former times remunerated by way of a hail tax which they collected from the farmers of their district without having to beg for it. Because he who did not pay the hail tax had to be prepared for the hailmaster's revenge: a harvest ruined by hail.

The dagger cult includes moreover a number of purification rites which come already close to regular exorcism. I will give one example: it is one of the dagger practitioners duties to purge magically impure places or buildings infested by demons so that a feast, perhaps a wedding or some other ritual event, might take place there without interference by spirits. The assumption now is that the dagger sucks up spiritual impurities or concealed adverse spirits thus rendering them harmless. Also the decontamination of food including meals in offering and medicines plays an important role with people of spiritualist ideas of hygiene. In this context the dagger practitioner will stir the food with the dagger. If it is a matter of flour, grains or liquids like tea or beer he will let the foodstuff run over the blade of his Phurpa (54).

Abusive Practice

In addition of these honourable forms of use are added those abusive dagger sorceries of which at least in past times people were often afraid. For this also I will give an example: a biography of Padmasambhava, who had perfected the Phurpa cult, contains the following story. Padma puts up in an inn asking the landlady whether she was sufficiently stocked with wine? He then begins to drink assuring the woman he would pay as soon as the sun was about to set. He drinks and drinks. But clandestinely he pushes his dagger on the dividing line between sunlight and shade on the ground. The sun now stands fixed in the sky and cannot go down. Padma continues to drink for days on end. The peasants now complain before the king: their harvest was about to be scorched because there was a foreigner (Padmasambhava was an Indian) sitting in the inn who had stopped the sun's motion by his Phurpa. In order to bring the matter to an end the king eventually offers Padma. to pay his bill out of the crown treasury providing he, the dagger man, would only pull his Phurpa out of the ground and let the sun continue its journey. And so it happens: Padma departs without paying (55).

The proper or fierce exorcisms have not very much in common with such picturesque legends. They are mainly solemnized according to rules valid for practically all highly developed rituals. They consist of at least three phases: nativity, crisis (in this context amounting to climax) and thirdly the dissolution.

The nativity (Werdung) is mainly to be understood as preparation. The Phurpa master invokes the Bud-

Wooden dagger (crystal decoration, brown ribbons) for the protection of threatened areas.

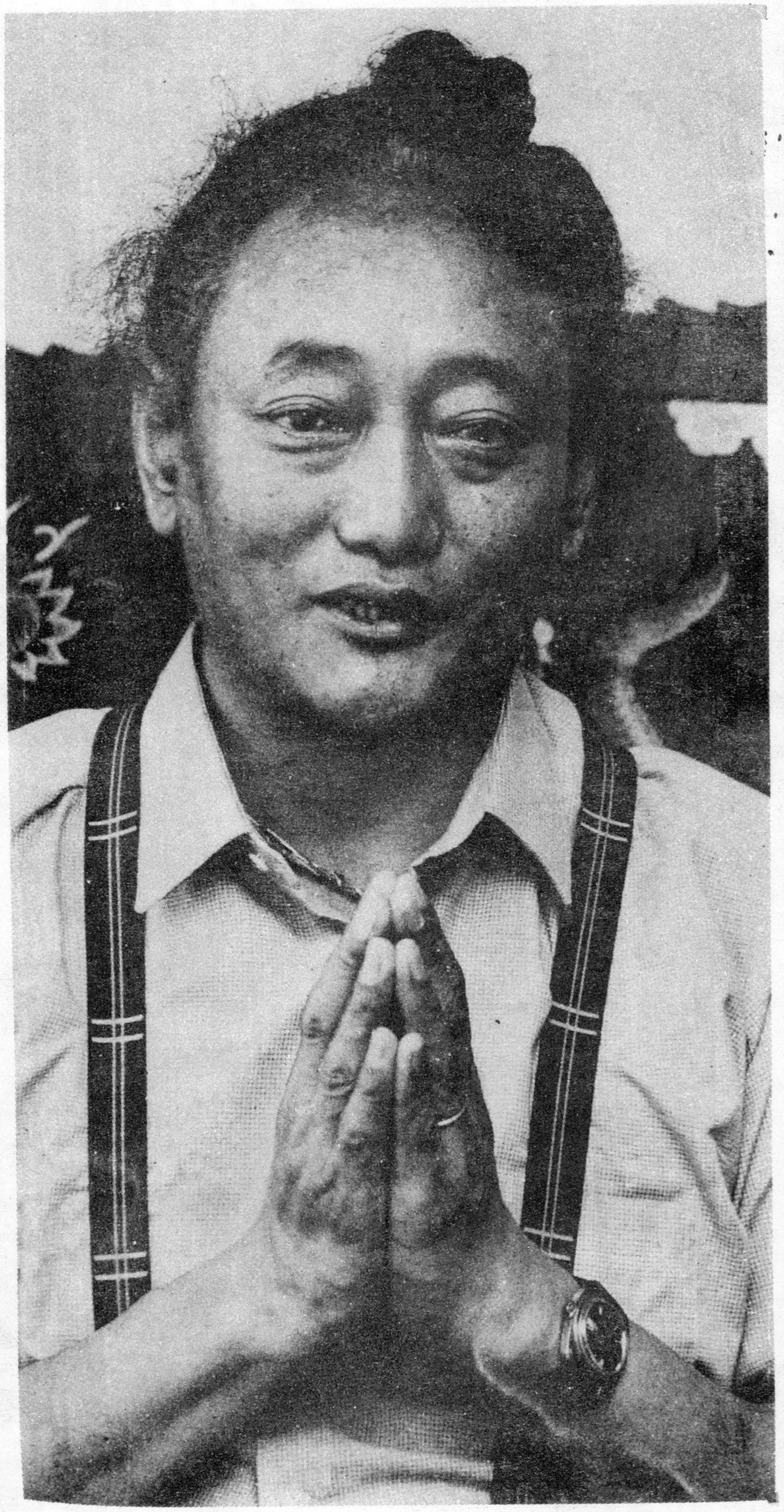

Phurpa practitioner.

dhas' and the gurus blessings and assistance. The Buddhas are all those who in past (and future) eons have reached complete enlightment, not just Gautama Buddha. By the gurus are meant all those sages who by tradition 'from soul to soul', by 'mouth-to-ear-whispering', or by their teachings written down as manuscripts, then hidden and later retracted, have handed down the ancient wisdom to our present time. The dagger practitioner, this also being part of the nativity, offers a sacrifice to the helpful deities.

The opening of the second phase, that of the crisis, is in the texts of the dagger cult occasionally indicated by the words 'you become Phurpa now'. This is to say the dagger handler now sheds his everyday personality uniting with Phurpa to become one entity with him. Thereby he acquires the power to fight the adverse demons. This union which cannot be explained as a process to the last detail is introduced by reciting the 'dagger sharp' or Kilaya mantra and is ignited psycho-motor-operated. The finally reached state of absence is, however, no trance in the sense of a loss of consciousness. One might rather speak of a profound concentration.

In the third phase, that of dissolution (Entwerdung), the dagger handler releases himself, again with a mantra or a sequence of mantras, from the state of oneness returning to the housing of his everyday personality. This metamorphic process, the dissolution, develops like the preceding nativity normally very fast and almost without transition. The phase of absence, however, lingers on for a little while: in the way of a self-forgetting elation comparable to a feeling one has after an exam passed. The ritual is terminated by thanksgiving to the Buddhas, the gurus, as well as the helpful deities.

So much as to the basic pattern of the ritual (56). As seen by the onlooker the exorcism ceremony falls into two main parts: the preparation and the actual ritual with the stress being clearly on the preparation. The dagger practitioner must create a suitable social environment. He has to gather his instruments, find a convenient place, and determine an auspicious date, provide for the music, supply the ingredients, produce the effigies, and prepare the 'prison', the yantra, where the adverse demon is to be jailed. These preparations can take a lot of time.

To begin with the social environment, the dagger priest can of course solemnize the ritual by himself and one gets the impression that such lonely exorcism ceremonies do not even happen unfrequently. But whenever such ceremony is performed by command, perhaps for curing a person, one will see the dagger man in company: there are the people immediatly concerned, like the patient and his relatives. In addition there might be helpers providing for the music (57), that is mainly the big handle drum beaten during the recitals, and who are responsable for the well-being of the participants: they supply the Tibetan tea, resembling a salty broth, so that everybody is kept on their feet. It seems even that the mere presence of well-meaning and understanding friends is promoting the emergence of the ritual work of art quite substantially.

Auspicious Times and Places

Now to the issue of auspicious times and places: when should dagger ceremonies best take place? This is mainly determined by the horoscope, by asking the stars. One also gains the impression as if Phurpa rituals, like so many psychically critical events, were best performed during the phase of twilight, at dawn or dusk, at times anyway when the ceremony is unlikely to be disturbed by incidents such as passers-by or tourists: the dagger cult has an aura of secrecy. Usually spectators are unwelcome. The place is often determined by the ritual's purpose. If there is a sick person to be cured or a particular location, a house, to be delivered from a demon dwelling there, the ritual will most likely be performed on the spot. Yet vicinity is no condition, distance is no obstacle and mountains are not in the way of its effect: when the British troops marched into Tibet from India and stood on the border in the Chumbi valley a great five day long exorcism ceremony was staged in Lhasa, the Tibetan capital, which according to Tibetan ideas, had to work over about 250 kilometers as the crow flies and across high mountain ranges.

Disregarding vicinity or distance there are especially suitable places of power which the dagger man should find. There are foremost the places of the dead. I am avoiding the word graveyard because in the Buddhist cultural sphere the dead are not actually buried in the ground. What they do is cremation which, though, used to the privilege of dignitaries for want of fire-wood. Then there is burial in the water which is mainly open to the inhabitants of the Tsang-po (Brahmaputra) valley. In Tibet there are no other great rivers. The general custom is the open-air-burial, the corpse being deposed at certain places. It will then serve the birds and beasts of prey as food. By this last good deed the deceased may yet gain some merit. That is why I use the term place of the dead.

Another location suitable for dagger rituals one finds in the temples in as much as they are built according to rule: Vajrayana temples are erected on rectangular The narrow side of the rectangle - and one usually finds the entrance there too - is oriented to the east. The two long sides point north and south. Now when you enter the temple approaching the altar about half-way and then turning left in a quarter circle then proceeding to the south wall the temple visitor will come upon a powerful spot, not in any way marked, which could be convenient for rituals. The stress is on: could. For in the last resort it remains to the dagger priest to sense the place appropropriate for the task by the aid of his refined senses (58).

Now some remarks on the dramaturgic composition of the ritual. Most magic ceremonies, including the Phurpa cult, are based on a largely invariable pattern, namely on the idea the magician-artist could in the great macrocosmic world trigger off events if only he presents or performs the desired event exemplarily in micro-cosmic form. This principle - the summoning of macro-cosmic events by their performance in miniature - is not entirely unknown to us: picture galleries and theatres breathe something of the power of what in ethnology is called 'analogy magic'. On the film-screen, on the stage, and in recent times also on the television-screen something is produced which - in as much as the piece corresponds to the rules of art - may not happen at once (unless in the viewers heart) but which in consequence of the performance gains a higher degree of reality and with it a better prognosis in the sense of the probability of its happening. Viewed like this art remains to be a problem of magic: its quality is measured by its power of conjuration. Vice versa magic is largely a question of artistic capability: will the magician

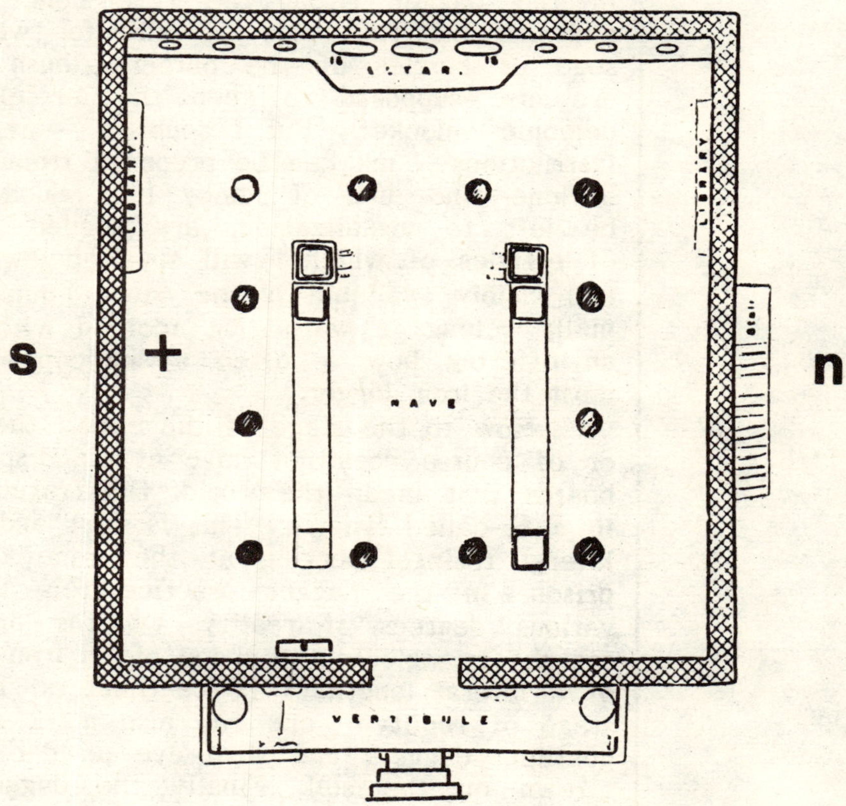

Ground-plan of a Vajrayana temple (after Waddell).

succeed in presenting his issue micro-cosmically so artfully that it really happens macro-cosmically?

In other words, a Phurpa ritual, similar to a play, takes place on various levels of reality. For example: the Phurpa manuals occasionally prescribe the dagger practitioner ought to sprinkle the place of the ceremony with blood or even with the 'menstrual blood of a dark-skinned Brahmin girl' (59). That could mean that the dagger man sprinkles real blood. But it seems more likely - because where is one to get a female Brahmin's blood in the mountainous deserts of Tibet? - that he manages with water dyed red in the same way as the blood shed on the stage does not come from the actors veins and as consecrated wine represents Christ's blood. Finally the dagger handler has a third kind of performance at his disposal: he visualizes the blood according to the principle already mentioned persuant to which the reality is not what is perceivable but what is imaginable.

Various Levels of Reality

This acting on various levels of reality becomes vivid also by the ingredients which the dagger practitioner must provide before the commencement of the ritual: the white mustard seeds - they are thrown to weaken intruding demons - cannot easily be procured in the Himalayas. They must possibly be imported from India (60). In the dagger ritual they are hence real, perceivable, and present. The same is valid for wild onions, caraway seed or berries of the barberry bush which, if thrown, are also supposed to keep the air clean of unwelcome demonic onlookers. But I doubt if - as is said in the old instructions - ink can be prepared from the cerebral blood of one who died of idiocy (61). Such inks, which must be left to visualization, are needed for the production of effigies of which I will speak below. What is apparent and visibly available is the cultic equipment. To this normally belongs a water jug adorned with peacock feathers, an offering bowl - often a skullcap - and last but not least the iron dagger.

Now to the stage of the event: the dagger practitioner of course does not have at his disposal the occidental boards that mean the world. His tragedy is enacted more in a so-called 'yantra'. This is first and foremost an equilateral triangel serving at the same time as a trap or prison. In the dagger practice this triangle appears in various degrees of reality. On the picture (p. 76) you see the triangle in the shape of an iron box with a lid and of a lateral length of 20 centimeters. This triangle - next stage of reality - one can also mark on the ground with guardian daggers and with dye powder of pulverized clay strewn on the soil. Finally the dagger mantric - next stage - is capable of producing the yantra in his head.

Before the Phurpa tragedy can commence one needs also an actor though. In normal life this is a harmless human being that professionally sometimes does the part of the king, then the beggar, the wise grandfather, and at times the juvenile lead. This function of the actor

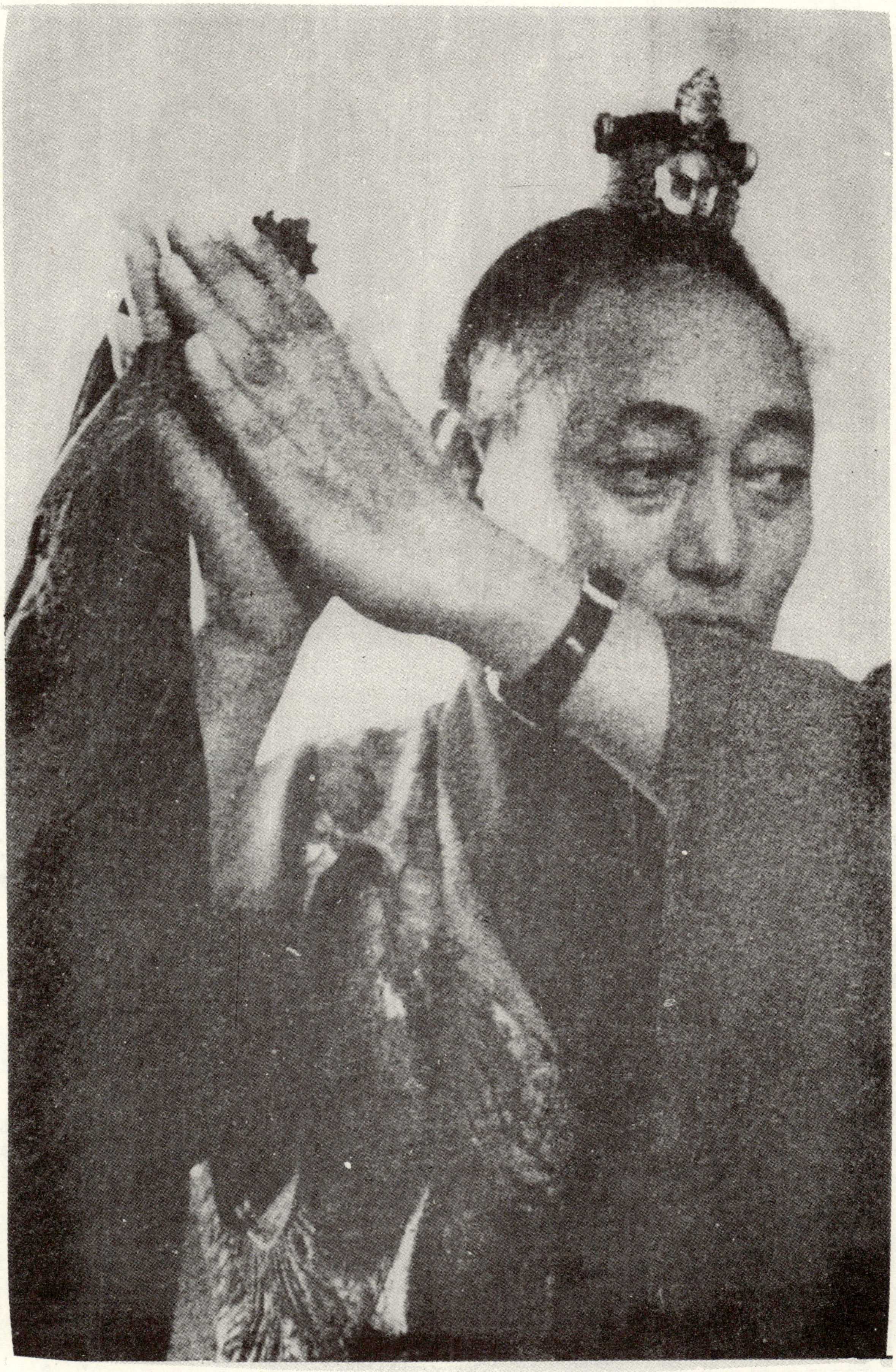

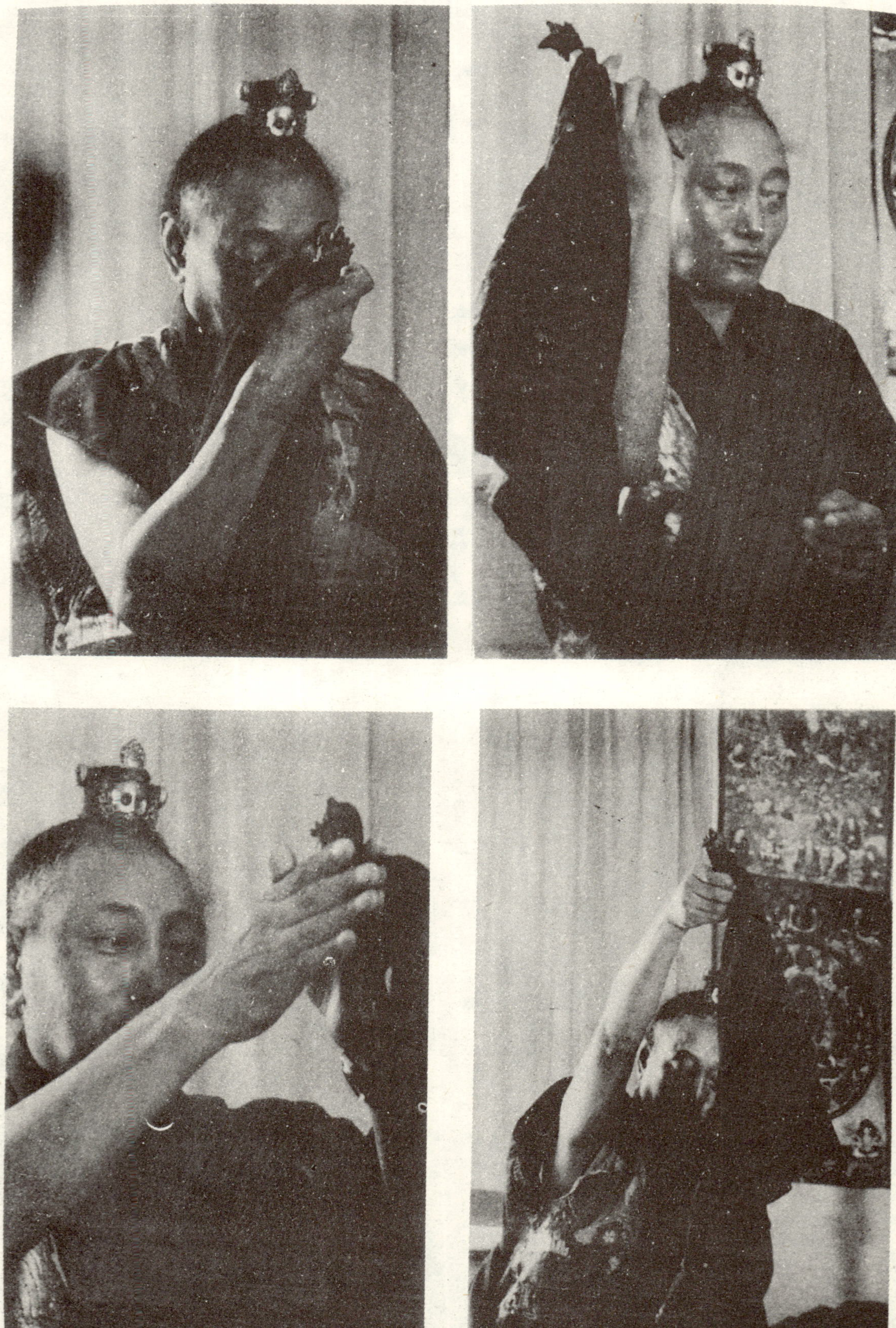

is in the Phurpa cult taken over by a 'linga' meaning as much as 'image' or 'symbol' (62). This image may look very different. It might be in the form of an about two hands high cone, not very much like a human, made of dried and then painted dough (63). This would, however, be the exception. As a rule the dagger man draws the image with ink, watercolour, or possibly also with blood on a piece of paper the size of a hand. Here you see such an effigy which like so many effigies represents an obviously unhappy man-like creature often chained.

Now finally the curtain may go up and give way to the other, the tantric space and time dimension. This may happen in all quietness but perhaps accompanied by the thunder of the handle drum covered green, by the whizzing sound of the cymbals and the wailing of a bone trumpet. Indeed there are Phurpa songs one may strike up. The Phurpa priest begins with his nativity. He then

Paper effigy (linga).

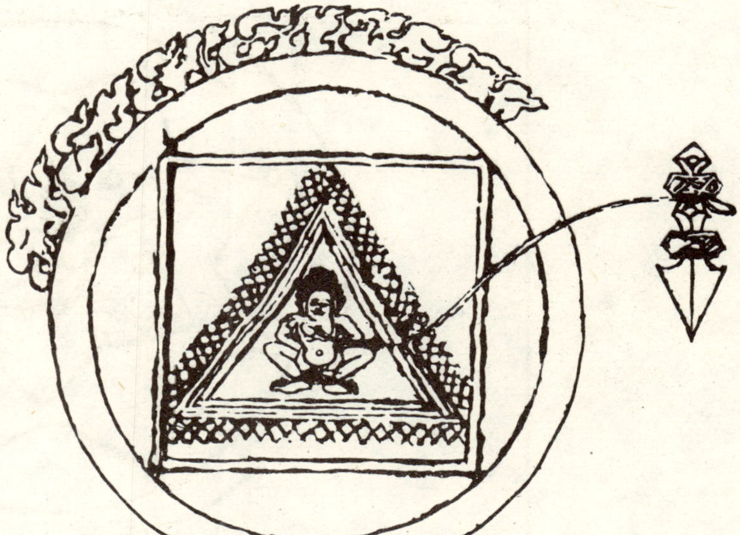

recites the dagger sharp Phurpa mantra. He becomes Phurpa, the dagger, the god, the dagger-deity, whose fine senses will in the following enable him first to identify the evil bringing demon and to localize it. The mantric syllables and the mudras join in a stream and the Phurpa master starts to lure the demon into the triangel, into the yantra from which there is said to be no escape. For a bait, for a lure he uses the paper effigy putting it in the centre of the triangle. This allurement, methodically the most critical phase of the ritual, may last an hour or more. The dagger man writes names and syllables for this purpose on the effigy. He sprinkles it with blood of varying degrees of reality. He rolls the dagger between his palms. He points it to the sky and to the ground and moves the Phurpa along with its black silken flag behind his back from the right into the left hand. He moistens the three-edged blade with water. Then he strikes: he knifes the effigy. He hammers it to death. He cuts the effigy to pieces. He again recites an igniting syllable chain. Finally he burns the remains of the effigy up and on the level of the perceivable the ceremony becomes extinct.

The Linga Mystery

Now to the level of the imaginable: who actually is the shabby little man on that piece of paper? In the sense of the analogy magic the effigy, the 'linga', ought to be the demon of misfortune which must be fought. And that is not incorrect. But it is not correct either. This impersonation of evil is manifold. Firstly it serves as a bait to lure the demon recognizing himself in this drawing thereby sort of pouncing upon himself, the effigy, and thus crashing into the prison of the triangular yantra. This is, however, only half the truth. Taking the opinion for granted that the reflex of a bodily creature - demons having according to the doctrine invisible bodies - is identical with what is reflected, hence identical with the demon

then the effigy would indeed be the demon itself. But who is the demon? Is it the demon of illness which is to be exorcised? Is it the demon of the person in whose favour (or detriment) the Phurpa ritual is performed? The truth comes round when one recognizes also the dagger practitioner himself in the effigy who offers himself for the sake of a sentient being, no, knifes himself and, as depicted on the photo (p. 94), directs the Phurpa'against himself in order to help someone else to luck. And furthermore: the image, that litle man, drawn with ink on poisoned paper, is you and I, all of us.

Dakini Power

What does a man think who by way of a ceremony and a ritual point of reference, the effigy, brings about an identity catastrophe in the course of which the misfortune in the disguise of a demon is destroyed? This question cannot be precisely answered. In the ocean of uncertainty one yet finds a firm island, an orientation, definitions and ideas here and there which emerge frequently in a

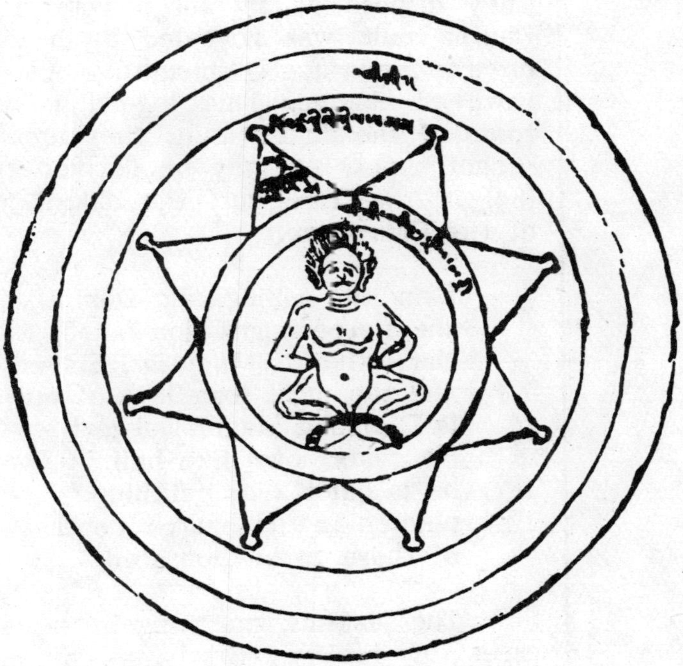

conversation. One of those is the word 'dakini'. A dakini is, literally translated, an 'air walker' or a 'sky dancer', a mainly benevolent female spirit or ghost whose main task is to establish the contact between the human world and the realm of the gods and demons and to keep it up. In Himalayan art the dakinis are often depicted: always clad with a loin-cloth made of skulls and human bones, young (it says they are all sixteen years old) and 'lion-faced'.

The dakinis take a heightened place in the thinking of tantrism adepts and especially of the dagger believers.

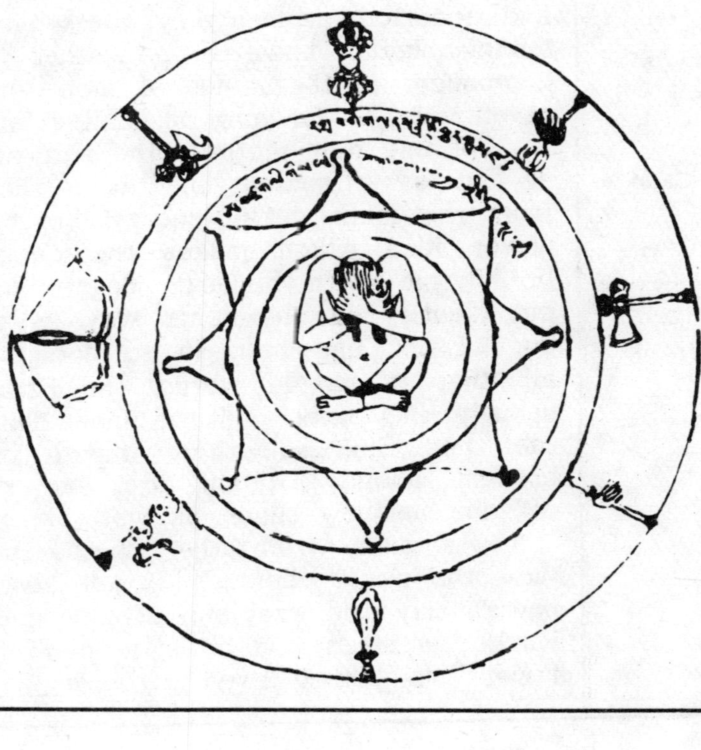

They dispose of special powers. It is said that the entire Phurpa cult was revealed by a dakini in a cave situated on the (mythical?) mountain Ya near the little Tibetan town of Samye. This legend is yet another hint to the roots of the dagger cult: they apparently go back to matriarchal times. As may be derived from the following verses (64) of the Tara cult the dakini is still today the mother of the Phurpa cult:

> I am the subjugating Dakini,
> the fierce angry lion-faced,
> the father is Manjushri Slayer of Death
> and the most excellent of our sons
> is Diamond Magic Dagger!
> He casts down like hail,
> he is quick like lightning,
> planted in the heart's centre
> of those to be liberated.

The dakinis must again be imagined in various degrees of reality: firstly as an invisible ghost but then also incarnated in earthly women who, thanks to their dakini power, are empowered to accord the spiritually educated man 'the three satisfactions'. The extent of dakini power - what is probably meant is the faculty to help the men to repeated personal renewal - seems to vary depending on the personality of the male beholder. Accordingly each man has 'his' dakini which he may recognize more in one woman, less in another, and not at all in a third. It makes comprehension more difficult that the dakini appears in five different impersonations each of which being assigned to the five constituents (skhanda) of the human body. These five dakini manifestations exist as five 'external' dakinis who sort of fly freely about and function as heavenly messengers. The five 'internal' dakinis should, however, be rather imagined as the female component in the minds of men similar to what the Swiss psychiatrist C. G. Jung has called 'anima'.

An Identity Catastrophe

If one now pictures the self of the dagger practitioner not as a nucleus but as a shell insulating the outer from the inner dakini energy one comes already near that power idea which makes the dagger man divine, namely Phurpa. With his iron dagger he pierces the shell of his identity in the same way as a chick pecks its way out of the egg-shell. In so doing he gains, I am saying all that in simple words, the Phurpa existence. Simultaneously the outer and the inner Dakini powers make contact and then something like a gigantic short-circuit is brought about, a light arc, an energy impact, sparking off the nativity shock as well as the identity catastrophe.

As seen from the Phurpa practitioner's point of view the ritual obviously is not always fun. The ceremony, particularly the problem of the nativity shock (Werdungs-Ruck), presents itself as a painful test which will not always be passed even after good preparation. A failure

Dakini (bone carving of a ritual apron, original height: 9 cm).

(65) leads to a loss of face before oneself and in front of others. One can also read about regular punishment, namely madness, in consequence of an unsuccessful ceremony (66). Dagger men do try - by the aid of specially made amulets against misdirection of the energy impact - to protect themselves against a psychic accident and the failure of the ritual. Yet there remains a rest of fear to fail and the dread that the evil bringing demon might perhaps win the struggle and the expected healing effect fail to come.

The Effects of a Phurpa Ritual

As to the effects: so far I have demonstrated the dagger cult uncritical of the subject thereby giving rise to the impression as if the effect was entirely undisputed, as if the dagger ritual would necessarily deliver a person from tuberculosis and avert an oncoming thunderstorm with certainty. Now what about these effects? If you ask if a Phurpa ceremony would be the suitable means to reverse the laws of nature, hence to enable a man to fly through the air, the answer is no. But is it really always a question of reversing the laws of nature? If you instead ask if the Phurpa cult was able to create realities in people's minds then the answer is certainly yes. Thus the Phurpa cult can move mountains and help to win wars.

For example: when the British, as mentioned before, invaded Tibet in 1904 the Tibetans organised in Lhasa a big damnation of the fair-headed enemies whereby one has not at least to imagine a great Phurpa ceremony. Coincidence or not: at the same time the British lost their yaks. Around thirty thousand of the pack animals perished from foot-and-mouth disease. This event now convinced the population that the then 13th Dalai Lama must have the stronger charm at his disposal and that the approaching columns of British troops were doomed to death. In consequence the Tibetans felt encouraged to cut the invaders off from their food supply and even to throw stones at their officers. But not enough with that. The rumour of the damnation and the perished yaks spread also to the east of Tibet: the Kham Tibetans living there, infamous robbers and cut-throats, consequently felt strong enough to shoulder their fork muskets and to rush to the aid of their otherwise not much loved brethren, the Lhasa Tibetans.

So the English advanced but very slowly due to their transport difficulties, supply problems, and increasing military resistance. Although they finally reached the capital Lhasa they had to return immediatly in face of the already menacing winter. And this in disgrace: the Tibetan regent (the 13th Dalai Lama having fled) presented the British general McDonald with a farewell present in the form of a Buddha statue remarking he, the English fire-eater, ought to improve and in the future live by the sublime, the Dharma (67). In other words: Though the dagger practitioners may not be able to see through the mountains, to fly or to let the water flow uphill they create, nevertheless, psycho-social realities which are effective. The same applies equally to curing ill people by the aid of a dagger: Phurpa rituals may exorcize illness making demons or not. This is not what matters. The dagger ceremony will - thus it is designed and arranged - leave a sick person not unimpressed and his or her condition not uninfluenced. The fashion and extent of the ceremonious attention do their work. Therefore, one cannot discard the dagger cult as without consequences.

With this the subject of the effects is not yet dealt with exhaustively. On the contrary the hitherto described old and magic Phurpa cult produces a side-effect which in today's modern dagger practice has advanced to the position of a main effect: the dagger cult, this being the vital point, may also be practised and arranged in so much a way as to substantially contributing to the dagger handler's luck. The reader should now be prepared for a sharp thematic bend. To point out its end right away: The Phurpa cult has produced two different rituals running side by side. There is first the old wrathful exorcism ritual described above which the dagger priest performs for the benefit of other people. And there is secondly a peaceful ritual which, seen from outside, resembles the exorsism to some extent but which in truth is based mainly on different assumptions serving also another purpose, namely the dagger practitioner's own happiness.

Let us for a moment return to the point of departure and to the defintion according to which luck is simply described as the absence of misfortune and this becomes manifest in the form of demons. We must now leave this defintion of luck and turn to a new one: luck is now to be understood as an experience of unity, as a state of perfect harmony and inseparability of man and his world. This state of existence - the basis so far remaining unchanged - is also no coincidental product, no 'equally ephemeral as well as rare state of having no wishes'. This form of happiness, this experience of oneness, is moreover systematically manageable; and this, too, by way of the dagger.

This second dagger ritual which I call the mystic one as opposed to the magic dagger practice is based on a simple idea familiar also to the occidental reader: if you feel disturbed and unhappy, nobody being quite immune from that, you can generally not exert any influence on your psychological well-being directly. Luck or happiness cannot be ordered to appear. Seen like that luck touches us indeed only by coincidence and seldom and we can but hope and wait for an unfortunate state to sooner or later change into harmony.

This fatalism toward the problems of arranging the inner world, to which I have pointed before, is far from those trained in tantrism. Maybe they have not achieved very much in the way of road construction and electronics, hence the arrangement of the outer world, but as far as the arrangement of the inner world goes they are surely the much better entrepreneurs. That is valid also and especially for the field of self-inducement and the establishment of blissful states of existence based on the experience that psychic conditions can be controlled if not directly then indirectly and be changed via the body.

Such indirect influences can on principle be quite simply achieved: whoever derires to improve his state of existence must first select a, initially unspecified, physical activity, e.g. praying rosaries which is still widespread in Asia and only recently fallen into oblivion in Europe. For this people in the Buddhist cultural sphere use no catholic rosary but prayer cords with one hundred eight pearls made of wood, shell-lime or bone. And then one recites no regular prayers in doing it, no Ave Maria, but one says audibly or inaudibly a mantra, a chain of ignition words like OM AH HUM (67).

Effects and Side-Effects of a Ritual

In so doing a psychosomatic interplay is set in motion, perhaps hesitatingly with the beginner yet immediatly with the trained tantric: by the body movement, in this case gripping the pearls and pushing them on the prayer cord while reciting the mantra, an initially perhaps only small echo arises in the psychic sphere. This effect is mostly strong enough to intensify and qualitatively improve the subsequent physical process of gripping and pushing on the the next pearl with one's fingers. This improvement in the physical field will in turn amplify the psychic echo. In the course of a recital round over a hundred and eight pearls a shuttle effect emerges, a back and forth, a process of optimizing between the external activity and the internal state of existence which not necessarily leads to an experience of happiness but, with some exercise, to increased concentration.

That much to the principle explained by the example of the use of a rosary. Such examples are many: whoever wishes to do more for himself and his luck should while using the prayer cord simultaneously walk around a dignfied building, a stupa. That is a cone-shaped structure, more a monument such as you may see often in the Buddhist countries. By that supplementary walking and pacing around (clockwise) the psychomotoric interplay will increase and with it the effect. I happen to remember these simple exercises, open to anyone, very agreably: like wandering round the big stupa in Bodnath near Kathmandu: a stream of amiable people walking around the stupa in the last sunlight, the prayer cords in their hand, passing by the small shops as one finds them in Asia surrounding many sacred buildings and pilgrimage places.

Such procedures and their effect on one's state of mind are not unfamiliar to westerners. We too experience the calming influence of daily movement chains provided they are complex enough and sufficiently trained. Think of pipe smoking the charm of which lies eventually in the activity of one's hands, of preparing a cup of filter coffee or of knitting and of crochet-work - all of these complex processes whose soothing effect also occidental people consciously or unconsciously use for the establishment and maintenance of their inner balance.

Challenging Body Speach and Mind

Rosary praying and circumambulation are, however, practices for 'householders' and other simple people. One must not expect great and lasting effects thereby. The effect grows, though, the more such exercises meet certain requirements: they ought to last for a certain time, an hour or more. They should, secondly, be of a rather complex nature, i.e. challenge the body, speech, and mind. Thirdly they should, this being self-explanatory really, contain an artistic element in order to strongly effect one's mind. This type of practice for the advanced disciple one finds not unfrequently under the great roof of Buddhism although they have no dogmatic connection with the host religion. The two best-known ritual practices are once more widespread in present-day Japan: ceremonial archery and sword fencing, at one time vital activities and taken from everyday routine of a past epoch which are now astranged to their original purpose. These activities, once devoted to the martial arts, have been given a secondary object which has attained the level of the main purpose: the achievement of auspicious states of existence.

This is similar to what has happened to the dagger cult. Such an ingenious process rich in variations and entireness, all this playing a role, is well suited to set in motion that psychophysical interplay and to bring it to the desired end, namely the experience of blissful oneness. But contrary to today's archery in Japan - now hardly anything but a sport - the fighting character and the idea of subjugation has not been forgotten with the dagger cult. Main and secondary object appear interwoven with the Phurpa cult and not yet separated. Its relative duration and the interplay of mantras and mudras difficult to learn render the dagger cult - also in its mystical form - indeed hardly accessible for the layman. The Phurpa cult is mainly reserved for monks and similar people leading a spiritual life.

This increased degree of difficulty, however, affirms and deepens the effect: a Phurpa ceremony demands such a high degree of concentration that the dagger practitioner is left with no margin for mental excursions into the past or the future. What is required of him is the unrestricted presence of mind. One may ask oneself if

this interplay of physical reason and psychic effect always leads to the right direction? The answer is yes with some reservations. People experienced in tantrism and in dagger handling often voice the opinion that merely learning the ritual, the process, would by itself produce the desired inner effect. Yet all tantric and dagger adepts study - is this contradictory? - their art under the supervision of an experienced teacher who is to save them from accidents, especially from temporary or even permanent mental disturbances due to psychic stress: such accidents are possible.

The Great Happiness

And what does it look like the 'grande fêlicitê' (68), the great happiness? The reply to this question escapes expression in colloquial terms and is certainly beyond the competence of the reporter. Therefore, a Phurpa expert of the 14th century, Bu-ston rinpoche, shall have the word in the following, by describing in his Tibetan fashion where the mystic ritual may lead:

> 'He entered the gate of initiation and began to contemplate. He gained possession of a body of form which was appearance and emptiness. He was without outer or inner, above or below, front or rear, before or after; he was unmade, unlimited, undivided; he was without essence in appearance, without bias in light, without defilement in bliss; his glow was the clear light, his nature unproduced, his prowess manifold. And in this realm of undifiled real bliss he saw the play, the residence and the residents, gods and goddesses, dakas and dakinis, the subtle and self-sprung understanding, the miraculous knowledge. All events, inner and outer, were the appearance of his mind, occuring as the prowess of his understanding' (69).

When reading these lines one may finally gain the impression that there must be worlds in between the magic dagger ritual with its sanguinary details and this mystic bliss of existence. But that is not the case. Between the seemingly different forms of cult one finds upon close inspection merely shifts of emphasis. Bliss here appears more in the way of fighting misfortune, and there more as a final point to achieve. The peaceful, the mystic dagger cult can do without almost any of the magic ingredients, without mustard seed and bone trumpets the howling of which often frightens the western listener. And yet of a sharp distinction, here there and some other thing there, at least the dagger believers would not hear.

Dogmatists may at this juncture point to the differing manifestations of demons: in the eyes of the dagger magician they come under the category of sentient beings equipped with a, if not always visible, body and mind moving in the circle of death and rebirth. The dagger mystics, though, identify the demons more with their own thoughts, with meditation obstacles standing in bliss' way,

A monk circumambulating a stupa.

but not with sentient beings who to kill would amount to a sin and a contradiction to Buddhist doctrine.'However, a distinct dividing line cannot be drawn here either.

What both forms of the Phurpa cult have in common is the idea of self-sacrifice in each case indicated by the mudra of knifing oneself. Both have in common the figure of the dagger practitioner - here the actively working magician there the seemingly passive mystic in contemplation. They have in common the three-edged iron dagger: for the magician it is the weapon, for the mystic the starting point of his object-bound meditation, and for both the key to bliss.

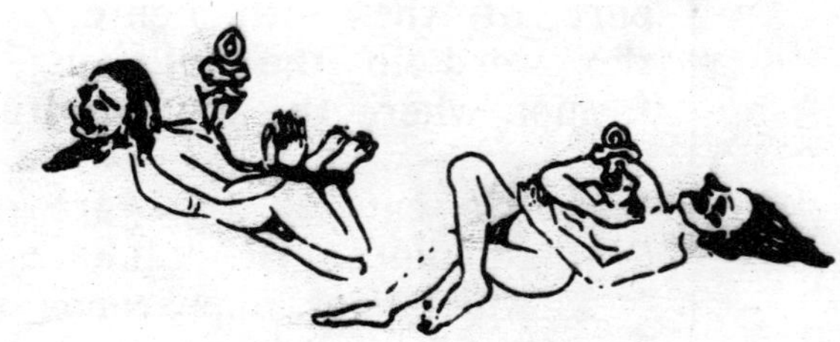

Dead demons.

The Treasure Texts

The Tibetan texts on the Phurpa cult now following move in their contents seemingly without transition between the pole of visible magic and the antipole of the ideated or visualized tantric world. The reader should not stumble over these thresholds but let himself be led through the entire undivided dagger world without concern.

As to the texts themselves some words of explanation may be added: they all are, as is also stated in the colophones, so-called treasure texts. By this we have to understand scripts originating from ancient times, in this case from the 8th century A.D. The texts were, it is said, hidden away. Later, in the 14th and 15th century, Ratna-glin-pa and other religious teachers have rediscovered these texts again (or visualized their contents) and written them down once more.

Part one consists of a table of contents of a manual for dagger priests rediscovered by Ratna-glin-pa (vide list of literature). The manual begins with drawings of patterns for making effigies (linga) and amulets such as one also finds depicted in this book. Part two contains the actual instructions. The chapter headings may convey an impression of what dagger pratitioners have to learn and which coordinates mark the position of the Phurpa cult. For the translation we have to thank Geshe Loden Sherab Dagyab, of Rheinbach (FRG).

Then comes, in second place, the translation of chapter 11 of the Phurpa manual by Ratna-glin-pa, done by Amy Heller, of Lausanne (Switzerland). This is a presentation of the more external process of an exorcism ceremony. The original Tibetan manuscript is damaged in some places. The meaning has been reconstituted, as best one could, by supplements put in brackets. To avoid misuse some of the mantras (here as in the other texts) have been omitted.

In third place follows a meditation instruction (chapter 15 of Ratna-glin-pa's manual). The translator of this is Imje Nyomba Natsok Kune Zakhan, of Kathmandu (Nepal). Contrary to Tibetan usage neither Padmasambhava nor any other Tibetan Early Father is quoted, instead a woman: the dakini ('air walker' or 'sky dancer') Yeshe

Tsogyel. She describes, other than Padmasambhava does in the preceding text, not so much the external procedure of a Phurpa ritual but more the beatifying inner effect upon the dagger pratitioner.

The fourth and fifth text, translated again by Amy Heller, has been taken from the root tantra of the dagger cult, the 'bhi-to-ta-ma' or also 'vidyottama tantra'. The two text excerpts published here may be found in the Kanjur (vide list of literature) under the heading 'Vajra mantra bhiru sandhi mula tantra'. It is here not a case of dogmatically neutral instructions but a recognized text of the Vajrayana doctrine. The demon Rudra therein mentioned, an early form of the Indian Shiva, is reputedly particularly baneful: Rudra knows the Buddhist teaching but has repudiated it now attempting to poison the believing Buddhists' souls.

Charm against eagles.

The Dagger Doctrine

Contents of the MS 'Most secret rituals for the invocation of the Phurpa for destructive purposes', rediscovered by Ratna-glin-pa (1403-1478).

A. DRAWINGS

1.) The wheel of protection of myself and others. 2.) Profound wheel of self-protection. 3.) The wheel of taming inimical demons. 4.) The wheel of taming and killing develish demons. 5.) The wheel of taming the serpent demons (Naga). 6.) The wheel of taming the deceptive demons. 7.) The wheel of inflicting and averting damage. 8.) missing in the MS. 9.) Wheel of taming the king demon and of protection for yoghurt and beer. 10.) Diagram for the protection of a place, a monastery, and a district. 11.) Diagram for the special ritual 'Wheel of handling the black-poisenous dagger weapon' (missing).

B. INSTRUCTIONS

1.) Benediction 'treasure of activities'. 2.) Essence of the secret tantric activity. 3.) Special and secret instruction on the subject of the celestial ladder. 4.) Last and precise instruction on the torma sacrifice. 5.) Especially profound exposition and enlightment. 6.) On the profitable instruction. 7.) Presentation of the great dagger ritual. 8.) Butter-lamp prayer on the completion of the ritual. 9.) Dagger mandala of the essence of the peerless truth (glorification by Mkhar chen gza). 10.) The unsurpassable mandala of the secret dagger in its entire purity and clarity. 11.) The destructive ritual act of the black-poisenous dagger. 12.) How to make effigies satisfying everyone (glud ritual). 13.) Meditation about the stage of imagination and perfection of the Jewel Chain. 14.) Presentation of the main ritual. 15.) The most secret peerless quintessence of Phurpa - Orgyen's sacred heart elixir. 16.) The ritual of the dagger-sharp activity. 17.) From the ritual (of the dagger-sharp activity) excerpted gathering rites (ganachakra). 18.) Invitation (directed to the patron-deity) to religious instruction. 19.) Invocation of the patron deity bse yi skyes bu, representative for all 14 Phurpa patrons. 20.) Very perilous request adressed to the five oath abiding worldly protectors. 21.) Ritual of invoking the substance void (yantra) of the god of death (named) Yama. 22. The wheel of the weapon activity of the black-poisenous dagger (sub-chapter to the ritual). 23.) Final ritual: taming the powers of the wrathful king. 24.) Defence of wrathful stones and tormas by touching with the sharpness of the dagger. 25.) Twelve-part and profound collection of various rituals. 26.) Wrathful mantras hitting like with a sword (by Sbriza Sbugu). 27.) Secret ritual activity with the treasure guard Ldong Lha. 28.) Especially effective defence of bad omen through the (protective demons?) rdor leg.

Paper effigy (linga).

The Destructive Ritual

THE DESTRUCTIVE RITUAL ACT OF THE BLACK POISONOUS DAGGER: THE RAZOR OF LIFE WHOSE RITUAL MAY CONFER DEATH.

Original authorship attributed to Padmasambhava, rediscovered by Ratna-glinpa (1403-1478).

Translated from the Tibetan by Amy Heller, Ecole Pratique des Hautes Etudes, Paris.

I as Padmasambhava have completely purified the mind by the Tantra (Sanskrit name) Phur-pa bhi-to-tama and I have perfected the practice of the Tantra of Thought (Dgongs-pa'i rgyud, one of the primary rNying-ma-pa Tantra). As a result of the breath meditation, the ritual of evocation of the deity is also (perfected). Having combined the many into one, it was buried as a treasure, making a solemn vow for the production of benefit for all sentient beings.

I, the glorious One from Oddiyana (Padmasambhava), have meditated in the rock cavern of Ya mountain on the mandala of the gods of the body and have empowered my own body by sixty Kilaya particles. Once the preparatory phases were in process, all the oath bound protectors offered the pith of their vital power. Following this, the pith of vital power of Phur-pa was also offered (to me). By means of one violent mantra, all functions will be fulfilled by relying on the iron Phur-pa. If you maintain uninterrupted (this concentration of power) whether walking, sleeping or staying, all obstacles will be prevented. The hostile demons creating obstruction will then be rapidly liberated (i.e. killed). According to the prophecy of the dakini, this is the vital essence of all gods and demons, the executioner of all the enemies of obstruction, the burning fire and the central axis of subjugation called (Phur-pa) bhi-to-ta-ma.

As you do not know (this text) as the root of the mind and heart, the hope of magic powers coming is by activating of the Phur-pa. It is like a bird in the sky pursued by dogs (i.e. It is futile unless you know the text)

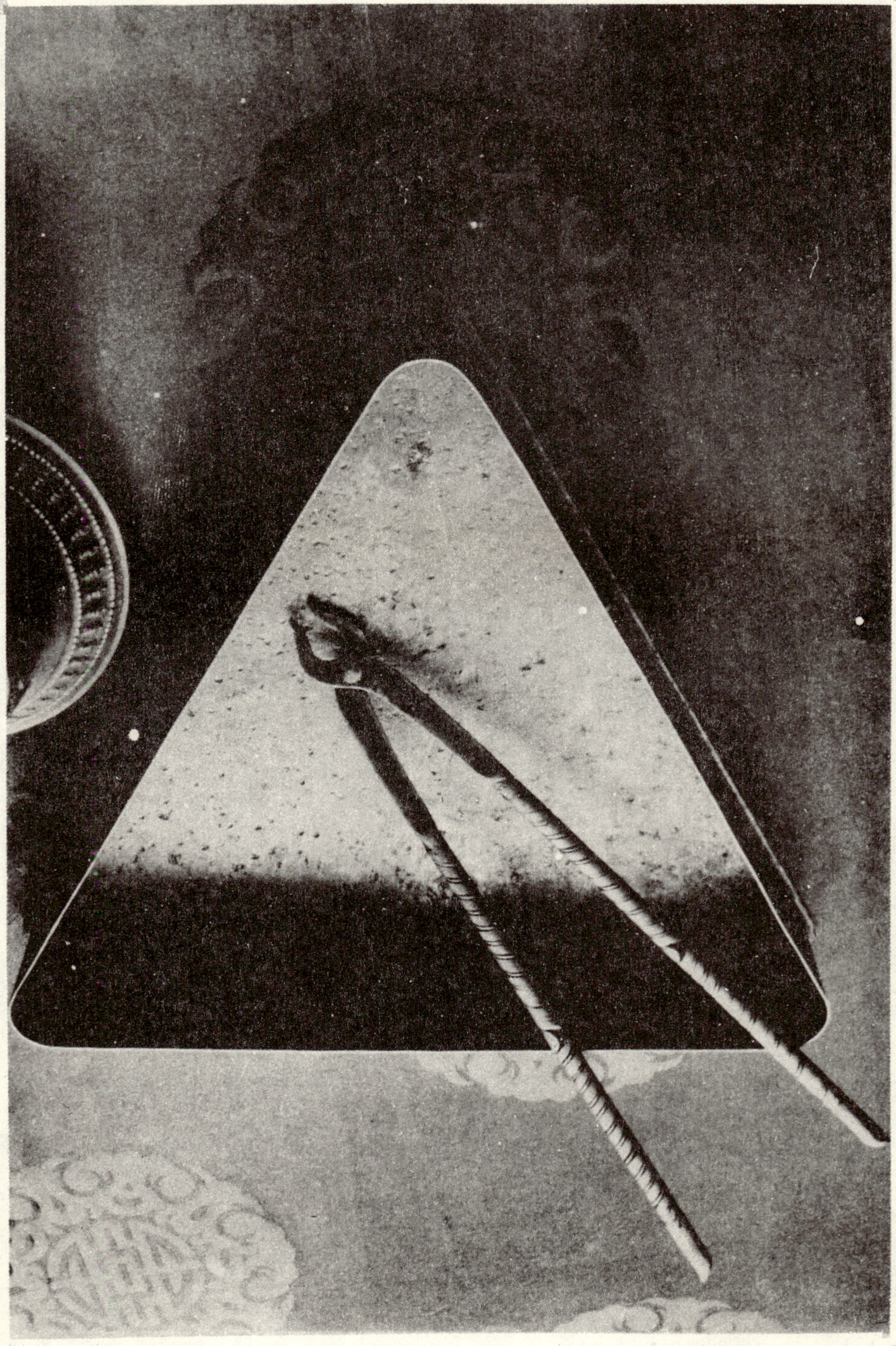

and so this violent mantra must be recited: OM VAJRAKILAYA... to the vein of the heart, to the vein of the vital forces, to the heart of the hearts. Recite this as a prolonged sound, making each one shake as if moved by fierce wind. It is appropriate to make 84 ritual recitations of this violent mantra and then the signs of the extermination of the enemies of obstruction will quickly appear.

Now, as for the explanation of the meaning of the mantra (as exposed in) the prophecy of the dakini: OM DORJE SHON NU Upon saying VAJRA, offer the developed mandala of the consort. Upon saying KI-LI, ten falcons. Upon saying KI LA YA, the ten wrathful gods and their best sons. Upon saying MA RAKMO, the goddess Lha-mo. Upon saying YAKMO, four female bse (spirits). For the vital forces, upon saying YAM YAM it is the long hand of the butcher. For the heart, roll the Phur-pa between the palms of the hands (to signify) the great female life-taker. For the vital forces, upon saying CHUM CHUM it is the life of the enemy. Upon saying TSI TA TA SOG, it is the master of life. Upon saying JA, it is the heart, flesh and blood. (Mantra syllables untranslatable). Thus empowering the iron Phur-pa, having meditated on the mandala of the gods, with concrete support in the linga (effigy) of the enemies of obstruction, liberate (i.e. kill)!

This was further commentary on the mantra with its root letters and all, which is the razor of vital force from the prophecy of the dakini, the magic power of the ritual acts of torment of all Phur-pa.

Now for the preparation of the circle of the razor of vital forces: OM VAJRA KILAYA. Upon saying JA it is the heart, flesh and blood. A TSI TI, A PA RA TSI. Recite while writing these syllables of the nineteen ma-mo and shen-pa deities (on the head of the linga). Recite and write right hand 26 (syllables) of the father-tantra. Recite and write on the left hand the fourth root of male and female spirits entwined. Bind the heart (of the linga). Write NRI (on the heart of the linga). Recite and write the mantra syllable NRI) on the right foot of the linga, then on the left foot. The iron Phur-pa, the mantra and the mustard seed now strike. At this time the hostile demons creating obstruction will be liberated. Thus it has been said in the prophecy of the dakini, as it appeared as the essence of the (Phur-pa) bhi-to-ta-ma.

Now, the commentary on the essential letters of all the preceding (mantra letters) which show the instructions: Firstly, concerning the meditation on the mandala of the gods of the body (and also) the meaning of the ritual which strengthens the middle of the three portions of the mandala. The sixteen KI LA YA grains empowering one's own body (allow) the start (literally: the approach) to realization as follows: OM VAJRA K LI KI LA YA SARVA BHA GIN BAM HUM PHAT JA HUM AH. After reciting this, the syllable OM will penetrate the sinciput. Then thirteen grains (marked) with the remaining selected letters (Ja). Then fourteen letters will summon all perfect-

<
Yantra (iron box) with tongs to handle the linga (paper effigy).

ion (HUM). Then fifteen letters which bring together on oneself alls perfections (AH). Then sixteen letters which absorb in oneself all perfections. And with the signs on oneself of OM and the three phases of JA, HUM and AH, offer the worship of the pith of vital power. These three (syllables) are the condensed version of the mantra of the razor, being the essence for stealing the life from its protectors. These three are the assembled essence of the gods of wisdom and the Phur-pa protectors.

Then there is the entire mantra of the the Lha-ma-srin deities and spirits in eight categories. Now, the meaning of this mantra is the three: worship, realization and liberation (extermination of the enemy). However, before the sixteenth mantra in this phase, make the ritual while reciting the long mantra already given. This will ensure the liberation through the concrete support of the linga's circle. The signification of the mantra on the five limbs of the linga was given previously. Now recite the linga mantra which gives the signals of liberation. Now it is necessary to meditate oneself as (Vajra) Kumara. Write concentratedly MI MI (MI means man in Tibetan) on the exterior of the linga, thus separating (it) from obstacles from the exterior. On the interior put the letter E, while reciting one mantra of the razor. Having (struck) the linga by throwing the ritual grains, the certain accomplishment will come. At this time, it is appropriate for the violent mantra to function and the signs of liberation of the enemy-demons creating obstruction will appear. By reciting the razor mantra as a piercing spear, the Phur pa will even soar, fly and fire blazes. Now at the same time the demons creating obstruction are liberated and the soul wanders.

As for the time of the wandering of the soul (bLa), the hide bristles and the hairs are distinct. If this appears in the upper hole of the ritual recipient, the soul is wandering. When it comes from the direction of the enemies, it is near.

As to the voice of the soul, it may assume the voices of various animals - yak, rat, goat, bird (in each case, an onomapoetic verb applies, imitating the sound of the animal). In all of these the soul may be found and then it is time to strike. If there are certain signs that it has become goat or game or yak, then strike with the iron Phur-pa mantra. It is explained that there are five ways of striking, However, (here) strike at the essence of the heart which links the mind and the body. Making the support the good and the evil inside the Phur-pa holder's mind, the holder is skillful. Spread liquid blood on the vein which is the place of the real NRI at the junction of the black and the white heart. Then strike there, joining the Phur-pa to the NRI like a light ray. Then, having absorbed it into one's own heart, thus capturing the life and vital force, make the life-authorization for extending one's own life. After this, the defilements become like a fallen tree trunk, and the NRI absorbs into the syllable HUM. Pronounce this noble HUM syllable.

Now concerning the heart residence of the Great Glorious One. By its fundamental basis, the punishment is rendered, and the flow of entourage will prohibit.

At the time of the ritual service, bind and cover the violent mantra, (and) one long mantra (is) repeated. During the evocation phase, appropriatly develop the name (of the person who is the target of the ritual). At the time of killing, (there is) the light of Mara. At the time of the wandering of the soul, the name (of the target) and the syllable JA (are pronounced). At the time of the separation from the life protecting gods, the NRI syllable and iron filings (are scattered). At the time of burning (the linga) recite CHE CHE JA LA RAM. At the time of subduing, (recite) CHE CHE STAM BHA YA. If obstacles arise, make the name of what is harming suffer.

Now the PRA instruction of the mantra (of) calling the name. Having first recited the violent mantra, then call the name. Call it until the very heart and the nine (orifices?). Call it until the vital force and the five (members?). Call eight times PHRIL and it resides in the vital force. For twelve, call it into the sacrificial cup and the flesh (of the target person). For fourteen, call for anger and cause putrification. Call it into the third vein and the noble HUM syllable. This being the fulfillment of the prophecy of the dakini, very quickly the function of the ritual acts will be accomplished.

For further progression of the veneration of the sixteen Kilaya letters of before, strengthening the essence which makes oneself Phur-pa and collecting the emanations together, from the heart of the triple mandala of clarity, generate oneself as Vajrakumara (Phur-pa) in a dark blue light ray. Arouse the heart of the one who is entirely victorious over the ten directions and having done this for the benefit of all sentient beings, arouse in oneself the genuine realization of the completely victorious ones assembled together. Meditate thinking of oneself as possessing the brilliance of this assembly.

Having made the veneration of the sixteen Kilaya letters, the signs of success will be manifest in three ways - highest, mediocre and inferior. As the highest sign, the Phur-pa moves (of itself), it strikes. Liquid blood and mucus appear, the butter lamps burn constantly, perfect absorption of thought into the object of meditation is also clear. Pleasant, favorable odours are perceived and so on. As the mediocre signs, one arrives at the continent of precious substance. The sun and the moon shine on the body and may be held in the palm of the hand. The sun and the moon are mounted. Silk banners wave. Trumpets are blown. Fire blazes. These signs will all appear on the Phur-pa. Last there is the continent of the blue flowers (to be reached). The Phur-pa soars in the sky. The ritual cauldron boils and sharp weapons are held. It is pleasing. Once all these signs have been perfectly accomplished and the recitation for the strength of the razor made, then other signs appear - dreams and memories of various armies, the separation of the linga, the act of flinging (the Phur-pa?), killing sentient beings, madness, throwing... (illegible), the chopping of wood and the holding of sharp weapons. As secret signs, the cooking to internally liberate the male and female ging demons (is done) and, having taken the substance of the internal liberation, it

Lama trying to kill a demon.

is eaten. There is the desire to pounce on the flesh of many hawks and wolves. The enemy is attracted and infused into iron (meaning into the iron Phur-pa). Eat the sacred syllable. Hatred is generated. Thus appears the prison (yantra) for the ritual union, in which the linga is infused into the syllable E.

To accomplish this, prepare the black soil of the cemetary, blood and various poisons and make the prison like the color of the sky. Write one time the letter E in the center of the ritual triangle and on the skin made pleasing by the hand of the executioner or (men of) evil sort. There should be smoke of gugu incense. In a bowl for the dried ritual pellets (place) white and black mustard seeds, wild onion pellets, shang flower pellets, black caraway seeds, iron filings and various poisons. Spread the blood of death (i.e. blood obtained by killing, not a blood sample) obtained by an evil disease. Empower the disease vapours and also the vapours from poison and weapons.

Having emanated the syllable E from one's own heart as oneself is Kumara (Phur-pa), in front of oneself is the door of the three sided iron prison. Elevate it to one side. Then underneath generate from one's own heart the syllable RAM, once red and once black. By fire, the vapours of a blue-red devil rise. Meditate on the iron prison from which there is no possible escape. Combine and reverse the threads of the evil E (i.e. make a little package of the linga?). Begin to reverse that which went on both sides. From one side, cast the ritual pellets. Write appropriatly on the outside of the linga (package?) and penetrate inside it (by mental force).

Now as for the form of recitation for the razor. There are twelve Phur-pa protectors, male and female ging and dud demons, male and female dakini, and several acolytes. Some are eating flesh, some are drinking blood, some are pulling out organs, some are separating the head from the body, some are holding the sack of diseases, some are making rain of weapons on rotten flesh with burning worms. (Agressively) like wild animals and wolves attacking flesh, think while crushing (the linga package) to powder. In the domain of the letter E , cut without interruption with the iron Phur-pa. Recite the prayers perfectly, and while doing so, roll the Phur-pa between the palms. The fingers make the mudra (tro po mo) of the fierce male and female protectors. The residue of the linga (package) is now burned. The protectors' mantra with the name concealed is now shown. (Mantra syllables in Sanskrit follow incorporating Tibetan words for life, heart vein, vital power, heart blood, flesh, incense).

Now for the necessary steps for the normal worship: On the body of the linga the heart word (NRI?), soul signs and all has been written. The triangle (yantra) is on black felt in preparation for the expulsion. The linga remains inside the triangle. Nine times do thus: Throw the ritual grains on the Phur-pa. Continue thus day and night. Meditate on oneself as Kumara (Phur-pa). Meditate on the entourage of Phur-pa. Meditate on the enemy, the vital force and the razor. Having acted in this way, the ritual act will be accomplished.

If one is a yogin, the ritual cauldron must be used in a cemetary. Then spread the poison, blood and charcoal inside it. Last, surround it by the brambles of the barberry plant. Meditate on oneself as Kumara. Spread blood and nectar on the iron Phur-pa. Burn gugu incense and fatty meats. While empowering the Phur-pa, generate brilliant radiance. Think of Phur-pa's entourage. To prepare the linga, draw the enemy with charcoals on Chinese paper, its forehead, bones, heart and name. Draw the soul to be punished with powdered clay. Spread what is appropriate for evocation on the feet. Bind it at the waist. Inside the evil offering cup (kapala), draw the diagram of the internal circle. Put it (the linga?) inside the skull (of the kapala?) and then place it inside the ritual cauldron. Cut the mouth. Write the secret vajra diagram on top. Hit the triangle in the middle. Occasionally throw the ritual pellets. Fling the Phur-pa. Having internally evoked (the god's presence) thus, in three months, the signs of success will come. The three precepts of the skull have combined to form a river (i.e. have compound effect). Subjugate it under the cairn-shrine (the pile of rocks in which the local deity resides). The enemy dies either by blood spurting or by knife.

As to final binding of the mantra of the razor of this magic accomplishment: SARVA AH NA YA VAJRA PHAT! TA THA YA THA YA HUM PHAT! AH BE SHA YA AH BE SHA YA HUM PHAT! And thus as the final signs, the accomplishment of the great esence is fulfilled.

Colophon: This is the razor of the vital force of the dakini's prophecy, coming of the essence of myself, Padmasambhava. The teaching appeared (to me) at the upper cavern of Ya mountain. This is the instruction taken from the tantra of the dakini's prophecy, manifest three times as the text of the highly secret razor. (It was) first hidden in essence by the celestial appointed master (Padmasambhava?), second hidden by the mountain of Confucius, and third hidden in the virtuous place of Bum-thang (Buthan). In later times at the rock cavern of Lhang-la valley, by both (Padmasambhava's scholar) Vairocana and (Padmasambhava's wife) Yeshe Tsogyel, as Padmasambhava's letters (written on) yellow paper. The ocean of destructive rituals of the black Phur-pa was hidden in the southern portion of the cavern of Khra-mo valley. May this weapon of liberation (be used only against) those who violate the regulations of the doctrine of the dharma-master and his descendence. Hidden as a treasure text with six sacred seals and revealed by Ratna gling pa at the cavern of Khra-mo valley.

The Peerless Quintessence

THE MOST SECRET PEERLESS QUINTESSENCE OF PHURBA: THE GREAT SECRET MEDITATION RITE: ORGYEN'S SACRED HEART ELIXIR.

Treasure text ascribed to (the dakini) Yeshe Tsogyel, rediscovered by Ratna-glin-pa (1403-1478) and translated by Imje Nyomba Natsok Kune Zakhan, Kathmandu (Nepal)

Homage to Vajra Kumara! In the highest meditation cave at Nēring Sengē Dzong in Mönka, Great Orgyenpa Padma Sambhava, with Namkhai Nyingpo of the Nub Clan, Könchok Jungnē of Langdro, Pelgyi Chonē, Queen Shelkar Za and the Guru's Consort Yeshē Tsogyel, revealed the Dorjē Zhonnu mandala. Success in the performance of the rite was heralded by the ritual Phurbas smiling, rhythmically dancing, their aureoles of fire blazing, on top of the mandala. When these extraordinary signs manifested, I, the Kharchen Queen, requested the thirteen most profound quintessential dharmacakras in the cycle of Dorjē Zhonnu.

This is the most secret practice, the ultimate quintessence; it is the elixir of the Guru's mind; it is like my heart, like my life itself; and of all the treasure texts of Tibet there is none like this. Therefore, the auspicious powerplace where it should be hidden is Tramo Drak, "Variegated Cliff" in the district of Dang-lha.

Although there are levels of instruction and practice in the method of accomplishment of this meditation, still it alone is capable of the most secret ultimate success.

In a solitary place where perfect circumstances exist, the proprietory spirits of the ground should be propitiated according to the Vase Empowerment.

The special superior mandala should be drawn with four "spokes" in the middle, ten "spokes" outside the four,

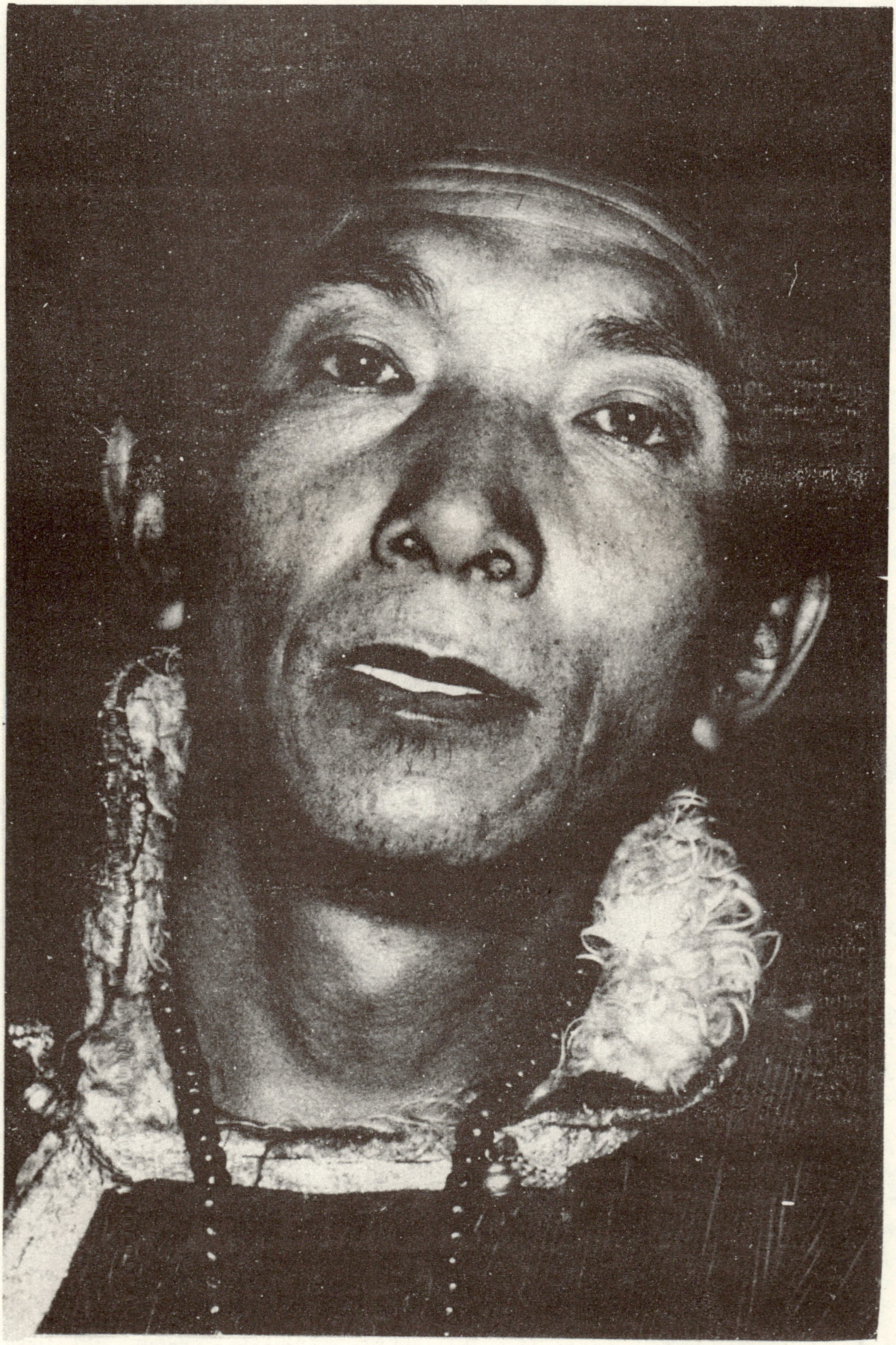

with doors and porticos, all within a circle that is the protecting wall.

Alternatively the yogin's throne should be made of human skin and the doors should be fully completed according to the rubric.

Again, as an alternative, it is correct to use piles of grain to represent the mandala, as they serve all purposes.

If the elaborate practice is the method of choice, the entire Lhaphur mandala is necessary; if the simple method is employed it is sufficient to depend upon a single central Kilaya in the middle of the mandala.

Regarding the glorious tormas and the various requisites for the outside and inner offerings, prepare them according to the rubric.

Furthermore, because in this secret meditation it is the creative and fulfilment phases that enrich and bring enjoyment o a mental level, elaborate preparation is not a major concern.

Take your seat on the throne of Bliss and visualise this dharmacakra. A blazing blue-black mandala-triangle surrounded by eight charnal grounds has as its centre+a vast conflagration, an expanse of blazing Awareness. Out of this Awareness the spontaneously manifest vision is accomplished: in the centre of an immeasurable palace without dimension, on top of a throne of lotus, sun and moon, and the four devils interlocked, a variegated blue-black HUNG magically appears out of the self-existent sphere of dharma, created spontaneously-originating Awareness; radiating and absorbing beams of light the syllable HUNG concentrates the waves of grace of all the Victorious Buddhas within it. Then the HUNG dissolves, and completely transformed appears as the Most Glorious Blue-black Dorjē Zhonnu himself. He has three heads and six hands, and his four feet stand wide apart in the proud stance of a hero, and his consort Khorlo Gyēdebma is entwined about him in a non-dual union.

The elaborate ornamentation of Phurba and his consort's bodies may be visualised according to the creative meditation of the Rite of Karma Purification (las-byang) or otherwise it should be visualised clearly and distinctly according to the Rite of Adoration (bStod-kyi-cho-ga).

On Dorjē Zhonnu's brow is HUNG-kara; on his right shoulder is Yukngön; in his throat is Tamdrin; in his heart is Shinjēshē; above his physical navel is Dütsi Khyil; in his gut centre is Miyö Gön; in his right thigh is Dorgyel; in his left thigh is Khamsum Namgyel; in his lingam is Topochē.

Generate these deities clearly and distinctly with their colours and their manual tokens as described in the Rite of Karma Purification.

In the heart centre, on top of a solar disc four finger-breadths in diameter, visualise a golden dorjē a single finger-breadth in height. In the spherical waist of this dorjē is the syllable HUNG surrounded by the thirteen syllables of this mantra.

Phurpa practitioner.

Further, clearly and distinctly visualise the syllable OM on the brow of each deity; visualise the syllable AH in the throat of each deity, and visualise the syllable HUNG in the heart of each deity. Then having established these objects of concentration repeat the three syllables seven times over. Thereby all the Victorious Buddhas of the ten directions descend here to bestow their blessings.

Visualized Phurpa deity (contemporary xylographic design).

The sign of empowerment is that the Buddha Amogasiddhi appears as a head ornament on the brow of each of the deities in the yogin's meditation.

From the HUNG in the heart of each of the deities rays of light emanate into Wokmin and the ten directions, above and below, and thereby the Awareness-double of each deity is invoked, and these Awareness-doubles dissolve into union with the Principal and the deities of his attendant circle. Through the same method, the Principal Phurba in the centre of the (external) mandala is also united with his Awareness-double.

To effect the approach of the deity, concentrate upon the HUNG in the heart of the deities surrounded by the mantra: beams of light stream out of one's own heart and vanish into the heart of the Principal, invoking continuity of the heart-samaya. Then beams of light stream out of the Principal into the ten directions invoking the core heart-samaya of all the Victorious Buddhas. By means of a white OM, a red AH and a blue HUNG, all the heart-responsiveness and blessings of the Body, Speech and Mind of all the Victorious Buddhas dissolve without hindrance into the three secret places of the deities. Finally, all the heart-responsiveness, blessings and power of all the Victorious Buddhas that have been absorbed into the essence of Dorje Phurba and his divine circle are absorbed into oneself.

After this visualisation and recitation, concentrate upon all the deities of the mandala, the Principal and the deities in their respective energy centres united in Father-Mother union of skilful means and perfect insight, standing like an open pod of sesame seeds , all murmuring the Kilaya mantra, sounding like a hive of bees - tiriri. The mantra-mala in one's heart reads:

OM VAJRA KILIKILAYA SARVA BIGHNAN
BAM HUNG PHAT.

Jup these thirteen syllables without verbal interruptions, keeping your seat constantly warm. The superior yogin recites each syllable 100.000 times, the average yogin recites the mantra 720.000 times and the lesser yogin recites the mantra 700.000 or 500.000 times according to his capacity. Maintain four sessions a day; or it is advantageous if you practice every day in accordance with the rubric of your Rite of Karma Purification.

If you strive in your practice of approach and identification through recitation and visualisation in this way the following external signs of achievement will arise: your Phurbas will beat rhythmically; they will float in the air; sparks will fly off them; they will bake the tormas; the Oath-bound Protectors will really bestow siddhi and perform their karmas according to their vows; your enemies will die; your rosary will burn your skin and your clothes; your saliva will be hot; and fire-light will emanate from your meditation room.

As indication of attainment of the Buddha's karmas you will experience the following internal signs in dream: fires will be seen blazing in your house and in the mountains; you will carry Dorjê Phurbas and Katvangas in your hands; you will see blue flowers blooming; you will fly through the sky; you will cross rivers; you will cleave great lakes; you will ride elephants and yaks; you will master all masked beings and the gods of the temple; you will strike black dogs and women; you will listen to the teaching of gods and demons; you will sacrifice your heart and life; you will carry sharp weapons; and you will wear good clothes.

As you grow strong in the practice of creative meditation these secret signs will appear: you will see the palace of the yidam deity and the yidam will reveal the future to you; you will attain firmness in the samadhi of fearlessness and the Bodhisattva's samadhi; you will accomplish whatever work you begin without obstruction; and unequivocal signs that the Buddha's karmas have been attained are for the superior yogin the actual appearance of the yidam deity, for the average yogin a vision of him, and for the lesser yogin a dream of him. Then practice the combination of accomplishment with action.

Then recitation to combine accomplishment and action as the Buddha's karma: generate the mandala of the deities above, and clearly visualise Glorious Phurba in his reality, repeating this practice again and again.

Then the approach of the Buddha's karmas through visualisation and recitation with the wheel of fire visualisation: by virtue of the mantra-mala as a wheel of fire, from one's face, which is as bright as a god's, light streams forth to the face of the Principal, to flow through his four focal points rousing and quickening the gods in their respective energy centres causing them to vibrate as the mantra's reverberations. Light then returns from the God's belly by way of one's own belly as above flowing through one's own four focal points to vitalise the mantra and its sound. Then again vocalise the mantra.

Then visualise a stream of light spinning off the mantra-mala entering the face of the god in a stream; rays of light radiate out of him into the ten directions, above and below, and you should imagine that the four Buddha's Karmas are being accomplished thereby.

Alternatively you should imagine that each of the four karmas is accomplished separately: pacification accompanying radiating beams of white light: enrichment accompanying yellow light: control accompanying red light, and destruction accompanying green light. Thus with intelligence and insight attain your objective.

Then rolling the essences of these four karmas into one, through concentrating aggression, arrogance and power, imprecation becomes part of your accomplishment. Recitation of the mantra that effects this synthesis, practised without verbal interruption, should be performed 100.000 times for each syllable by the superior yogin, 70.000 or 50.000 times by the average yogin and 30.000 times by the inferior yogin.

OM VAJRA KILIKILAYA DZA HONG BAM HO:
KATAM KAYE: JAYE BHIJAYE: ACHITE:
APARACHITE: MARA SENA PRAMARA TANAYE
SARVA BIGHNAN BAM HUNG PHAT!

This mantra should be recited with purity in a low murmur. During the period of practice these dream-signs should manifest in succession: building a palace, wearing armour, fire burning, cutting wood, waves rolling, demon-enemies killed, carrying sharp weapons, etc. These signs of aggression are the same signs that indicate the close approach of the deity.

After that, the attainment of approach through visualisation and recitation that accomplishes the purification of karma: after identifying oneself with the most Glorious Father-Mother union of Phurba and consort, light spinning off the mantra-mala as above flows through the Father dissolving into the Mother, quickening her four focal points of energy; then passing from the Mother's "sky" into the hole of the Father's dorjē this light turns the mantra-mala; and finally beams of light radiate from the

Phurpa priest and Dakini (from a Phurpa pratitioner's handbook).

mantra, bestowing the four Buddha's karmas, and this should be visualised clearly, as above, while you repeat the mantra 10.000 times.

Thus the approach, accomplishment and karma purification, these three, completed, the measure of attainment is as follows. At this point whatever aspect of the four Buddha's karmas you require will be manifest and you are identified with the qualities of the Yidam Deity who possesses the supreme siddhi. In the third bardo you will attain a vision of the deity and without any doubt whatsoever you will attain the level of Dorjē Zhonnu in the sambhogakaya. I, Karchen Za, give my solemn promise that this will be so.

Then the final proceedings: complete the meditation with the dedication of merit and prayer of aspiration. It is best if you can continue the practice of approach and accomplishment ever after like the flow of a river. If this is not possible you should take one week out of each year for its practice. Alternatively, you should practice the meditation once evry day without fail.

This quintessence of Great Orgyen's heart is the+single most essential meditation practice of Kharchen Za. At some time in the future may it fall into the hands of a righteous spiritual successor. SAMAYA: KHATAM: GYA GYA GYA.

This treasure-text was removed from the Tramo+Drak in Dang Lung (lDan-lha in the text) by Ratna. This is a faithful copy of the third-generation redaction of the yellow-paper manuscript.

This Phurba Drupchen, taken from the Phur ba yang gsang bla med don gyi snying po las rgyab chos smad las dug phur nag po'i mtshon cha las kyi 'khor lo, a terma of Ratna Lingba, has been translated from the cursive Tibetan manuscript into English by the Imje Nyomba Natsok Kune Zakhan, and finished on the fifth day of the dark of the sixth moon of the wood-ox year. May those whose good fortune have led them to read it find the indipensable master to give them authorisation, initiation, and detailed explanatory meditation instruction, without which this Drupchen is meaningless or dangerous. Thus prepared, may this practice bestow Dorje Phurba's siddhi and bring light and happiness to all beings everywhere. SARVADA MANGALAM.

The Root Tantra

VAJRA MANTRA BHIRU SANDHI MULA TANTRA (The Root Tantra Assembling the Fierce Vajra Mantras), Kanjur, Peking Edition, vol. 10, no. 467.

Translated from the Tibetan by Amy Heller, Ecole Pratique des Hautes Etudes, Paris.

Chapter 5: The objective of the meditation on liberation

Then Vajrapani said: This is the great necessity, the core meaning of the very Dharma (Buddhist Law) which is un-born and un-produced from all eternity. Before proceeding to liberate Rudra (name of a wrathful demon) from suffering and pride by the actual perception of the (components of) the ego, the means, discriminating wisdom and compassion must all agree. Then the one who demonstrates those three manifestations of mind will liberate Rudra. Having genuinely practiced (the ritual act) without examining the absolute meaning, (Rudra) will fall into the circle (of rebirth). But if the ritual acts are practiced by those who have perceived wisdom, then sentient beings are liberated in noble and pleasing fashion (i.e. beyond the circle of rebirths). Having perfectly achieved the assembly (of the deities and Buddhas) the three Buddha-bodies are obtained (Dharmakaya, Sambhogakaya, Nirmanakaya: Body of the Buddhist law, Body of bliss, Body of manifestation). Thoroughly contemplate the components of the soul, and prepare the ritual manifestation to crush (the components of the soul) by violent force. In order to subdue and assemble them under (one's) power, I and the teachers have explained the tantra (text) of assembly by means of mundane ritual acts.

The knowledge-holding practitioners in cemetaries which are celestial space prosternate to the meaning of the Buddha's doctrine, and praise it when there is risk of much degeneration. Just as virtues and defects (arise spontaneously) so will appear the dharma of contemplating the piercing ritual acts. Once this doctrine of frightening and evil ritual acts has liberated (Rudra) by the force of the violent mantra, then the perfection of obtaining Buddhahood will come. This is the manifestation of residing in the mandala: the gods, the mantra and the highest meditative concentration. These ingredients become matter and substance. The linga-figurine is the support of concentration. The name and family lineage (written on the linga) and the ritual tablets are the supports of the circle of the soul, life and the conscious principle (metaphor adapted from the circle of rebirths in six categories - human, animal, titans, gods, hungry ghosts and hell beings). By guiding the obstructive (forces), they will be prevented

Vajrapani.

(i.e. if the ritual is properly conducted, any obstacles+that might arise will be prevented). The messengers will make the realization of all the ritual acts. The glory of the mantra and the ritual ingredients are to be (mentally) produced. Then the ingredients intoxicate (Rudra) and the weapons fall like rain, silencing (Rudra) and crushing (Rudra) into dust. (Rudra) falls ill and from (his) heart, the practitioner is led to completely separate and eradicate the protective gods (on the head, arms and legs - these are the gods which protect the entire entity; when they are separated from a person, or being, then the conscious principle may be separated from the body) as shown by the blood on the head of the linga (at this point in the ritual the linga's head is coated with blood to symbolize its total incapacitation). The sesame seeds and mustard grains symbolize the constituent elements (of Rudra) which are assembled on the grooves of the phur-pa, to cut and burn (the linga). Having thus totally destroyed the support of concentration (the linga) the practitioner's complexion takes on many colours (i.e. pale or flushed with emotion). By the four ritual acts (appeasement, multiplication, expulsion or submission of hostile forces, and violent actions) suffering arises like the very essence of virtue and sin (which are identical in the absolute). The conscious principle is liberated beyond (the circle) of the soul and life. By the manifestations of HŪM and PHAT (syllables written or pronounced by the practitioner) the conscious principle is purified and advanced (in its karma, as it is freed from any residue of previous evil). The practitioner now mentally imagines himself as the victor over the ten directions (E, S, N, W, the intermediary points of the compass, the zenith and the nadir). Any remaining aggregates are purified by the three supports (the Buddha's body, teachings, and compassion) which represent the Dharmakaya. In so doing, make the benediction for the Buddhas of the past, present and future and their emanations. Thus it is ordered.

Chapter 7: Preparation of the fierce mantra and maledictions for each wrathful deity

Then Vajrapani taught the violent mantra and malediction for each. First, the violent mantra of the dud (category of demons) to destroy the aggregates: Put the figurine at the heart of black crystal in a skull bowl for the best black barley beer (chang) and wrap the figurine in black clothes used in a cemetary. Bind it either with black or many coloured strings. Make the iron knife enter the innermost life vein of the figurine. Take white mustard grains, black mustard grains, black sesame seeds, caraway seed, copper filings, iron filings, stone filings, poison blood and mucus and similar ingredients and put all of them into the skull. The mantra directs the vital force of the demon: Black demon ... (mantra syllables). Blow on the heart of the linga figurine which is the heart of the enemy. Bind the NRI (syllable written on the linga), make music and open the linga. Cut it to liberate the demons (to a better incarnation). Make the gtorma (sacrificial cake) for the demons and bind (them) by binding the BAM (syllable written on the linga). Pronounce PRAM to summon the mantra of the enemies, then TRUM, visualizing thus an island of agitated darkness, where the syllables are the speech of the demons of the future, and pronouncing these syllables, throw the grain ingredients to the innermost place. Whatever has been visualized will be quickly taken from the vital force by the demon: a black man with armour and weapons and a black mantra, a girl and a stone, a black dog, a black horse, a black bird and a wild black animal, a black bear, black crystal, and a black mountain, black lake, black crystal - all these in agitation and fighting. Visualize these, and oneself as the master of flesh, murder and instruction and there will come signs of the realiza-

The mudra of
self-sacrifice.

tion of the ritual acts. Then the linga figurine is hit and liberated. Hit it with knives, weapons, and phur-pa daggers. The remainder should be prepared with nectar, flesh and blood. Give black ku-ku (dog flesh) as food for the linga mixture. Sound the music and Rudra will be as intoxicated and once his consciousness grows dim, there is death.

Second, there is the violent mantra of Yama, the lord of death. Utter the syllables and make them enter the heart, throwing the ritual tablets and grains. Mantra syllables... to call Yama and his hordes. And visualize them accomplishing the ritual acts. The skull and the heart will appear to fly, as signs that the meditation is effectively liberating. Then the spell of the angry demons: call for the mantra and the names of all that have been visualized and make these reside in the heart and skull of rapid death. Wind the linga with silk the color of poppies, and dark red-purple thread. Open the mouth of the linga. Call the spell of the powerful liberating forces with the mantra. Call the mantra to kill the demons with the NRI syllable (Mantra syllables). Throw the ritual pellets while reciting the curses. The black man and the group of murderous deities are called to accomplish the ritual acts and quickly liberate the essence of the enemy.

Third, the violent mantra of the wrathful yaksha (category of demons): Take a white horse's heart and skull and make the linga figurine the object of meditation and visualization. Recite the mantra. Once these ingredients have been purified, offer the various liquids in the big brass plate and recite the heart-syllable of the yaksha. As signs that the ritual acts are being accomplished, the sound and light and names arise together. Red winds and snowstorms come. Hit the linga fiercely with the secret ingredients, then burn the remainder and throw the rest to the wind.

Fourth, the mantra of the fierce strong deity: in the heart of a divine white yak write the name, clan and the representation of the enemy to be visualized. Attach dark red thread to the neck of the linga and place it in a skull of noble provenance. Bind it with white silk, and various colored threads, attaching feathers from a vulture and bird of prey. To penetrate to the vein of vital forces, pierce it in the centre of the ritual circle. The circle is delineated by arrows for the four cardinal points and in the center, there is a triangle. Make the three divine stones of the hearth (fire) remain in the skull. Take the appropriate ingredients, the pure ritual tablets, the sharp weapons to make the form of the white tower. Now for the arrow ritual of the white mustard seed mantra: make the normal offering of the ritual ingredients. Throw them into the heart of the mantra. By the strength of the glorious Vajrapani, the numerous mantras of all deities united are recited (Mantra syllables) The enemy is beckoned to come and is liberated. As for the signs of the accomplishing of the ritual acts: the king, the chief and their descendants appear and are banished. The weapons chop the linga and then it is burned in the fire.

Fifth, for the crushing of the linga figurine: penetrate the skull with the divine support of the gods or destroy it on the ground as the residence of the great gods of the soil. The worst pestilence of the gods comes to the enemy, by the recitation of the mantra of the mamo deities who are the masters of illness. Make the accomplishment of the ritual acts by penetrating the skull in which the linga remains, having been bound by the five threads and covered with dark blue silk. It is in the center of a triangle inside a blue circle (mandala). Having pierced the linga in the skull, with its heartblood of purple-black color make the offering to the mamo deities and their assistants. Hit the neck (of the linga) with white and black mustard seeds and the usual ingredients for violent ritual acts, while reciting the mantra which is the curse of the numerous mamo deities. (Mantra syllables). By visualizing the syllables of vital forces of the mamo deities, evil will be destroyed by an iron knife. Make the mantra which is the names of the mamo and visualize their assembly along with black birds and wild vultures who take the flesh and the head. If correctly contemplated, the practicant will be able to visualize the heart as flying. As for signs that the evil has been destroyed, hit the linga figurine in the heart with the phur-pa, then with poisonous wood make a fire offering and visualize it as thrown to the enemy. Crush the remains of the linga figurine into dust and bring it to a cemetary. Thus the evil is destroyed and the conscious principle is liberated.

Now for the mantra of the violent za deities: make the linga reside in the center of the skull which is black. To reach the vein of the vital forces, put the iron knife to the linga and throw white and black mustard seeds, copper and iron filings while reciting the appropriate mantra. The mantra is the weapon to strike the linga while making the three red and three white offerings (the white offerings are milk, curds, and butter) and pellets from rotten meat and blood. As if surrounded by the sun and moon, the black envoy will come and the great snake with wings slithers. In the intermediary realm between celestial space and the earth, a rainbow will appear and the enemy will be induced to come. The vulture and the wild animals will destroy it. As to the essential meaning: the signs of the total destruction are shown by the offering of music as the heart and the intestines of the linga figurine burn in the ritual fire. Throw the normal ritual ingredients to the realm of the gods. Hide the skull in the earth which is the home of the klu deities. Hail will fall. Destruction will be instantaneous. The mouth becomes mute. The arm and leg become stiff.

Now for the violent mantra of the mischievous klu deities: in an isolated place at the juncture of three valleys make a blue-black tower with grains inside a triangle. On the head of the linga write the name and clan of the enemy. In the receptacle for purification (the skull cup) place the three white offerings as before and the three sweet offerings (molasses, honey and sugar) to the klu and nyen deities. Recite the mantra and the great fire burns, the great water flows. The bull, the ox, the frog, the snake, the bear and the scorpion assemble, the wood is chopped and the earth crumbles. On the ritual tablets thrown in the direction of the klu (i.e. to the ground) visualize the separation of the aggregates without any remainder, and the enemy dies by leprosy or melancholy. Thus it is ordered that by the fierce mantra of each of the categories of wrathful deities, all suffering as karma created in the phenomenal world will be transformed.

Colophon of the entire text in eleven chapters: This is translated by the great master from India, the guru Padmasambhava and the Tibetan translator Vairocana at the request of the Tibetan King Khri-srong lde-btsan (reign: 755- ca. 795 A.D.).

Acknowledgements

This book could not have been published without the friendly assistance of knowledgeable experts. For their support the author wishes to thank foremost Lama Sherab Gyaltsen Amipa, of Rikon (Switzerland), Khenpo Rinpoche Yeshe Chödas, of Menton (France), L.S. Dagyab Tulku, of Rheinbach (FRG), Lama Kunsang Dorjee, of Rikon (Switzerland), Keith Dowman, of Chabahil (Nepal), Dr. Edelgard Gramberg, of Wiesbaden (FRG), Amy Heller, of Lausanne (Switzerland), Geshe Samten Karmay, of Antony (France), Dr. Hartmut Kiock, of Munich (FRG), Dr. Ing. Gustav Lennartz, Thyssen Edelstahlwerke, Krefeld/Witten (FRG), Dr. Helmut Eimer, of Pützchen (FRG), Prof. Siegbert Hummel, of Röthenbach (GDR), John C. Huntington, of Columbus/Ohio (USA), Geshe Takung Khedub, of Rikon (Switzerland), N. Grupo Ronge, of Königswinter (FRG), Hans Roth, of Bad Münstereifel (FRG), Dr. Hans Wolfgang Schumann, of Vinxel (FRG), Geshe Pema Tsering, of St. Augustin (FRG), Lama Sonam Phun Tsok, of Pharping (Nepal), as well as a number of other helpful informants.

Notes

(1) A summary of the empirical research into luck and happiness and its results may be found in Noelle-Neumann, Elisabeth: 'Politik und Glück', in Baier, Horst (editor): 'Freiheit und Sachzwang - Beiträge zu Ehren Helmut Schelskys', Opladen/FRG 1977.

(2) The ritual daggers has many names. Tibetan terms are: Phur-pa, Phurbu, Zer-bu and Dorje Zhonnu. Sanskrit terms are: Vajra Kila, Kilaya, Karma Kila, and Vajra Kumara.

(3) Huntington, John C.: 'The Phur-pa, Tibetan Ritual Daggers', Ascona/Switzerland, 1975.

(4) Photos immediatly connected with the Phurpa cult may be found in Hoffmann, H.: 'The Religions of Tibet', New York 1961, and Rock, J. F.: 'The Amnye Ma-Chhen Range', Rome 1956. The photo in Rock's book shows a Bön priest who, as Rock reports, had come to his house and posed for the photograph on the flat roof of his house and this along with his utensils, among them also a Phurpa. The photos in Hoffmann's book have presumably also been arranged.

(5) A hint to the existence of the Phurpa cult in Japan can be seen in the way of a wooden statue (19th-20th century). It represents an old man killing a demon in the disguise of a baby with a three-edged dagger (Kyoto Gallery Tony Camert, Brussels 1985).

(6) The areas of the (Tibetan) Vajrayana Buddhism and the dagger cult are largely congruent, though not completely so. On the one hand the dagger cult may also be found among non-Buddhists like the followers of the Bon religion. On the other hand there are many Tibetan Buddhists, such as the members of the Gelugpa or yellow-cap sect who mostly reject the Phurpa cult.

(7) The origin of the dagger cult from Mesopotamia has been documented by Siegbert Hummel, of Röthenbach i.V. (GDR), in several publications (vide list of literature). According to Hummel's findings the ritual daggers must be regarded as guardians, boundary-posts, and magic traffic signs barring the demons' way. This opinion is corroborated by the practices of Tibetan weather-makers: they surround fields threatened by thunderstorms with wooden Phurpas stuck into the ground. For this see Klaus Chr.: 'Schutz vor Naturgefahren', Asiatische Forschung, vol. 97, p. 310, Wiesbaden 1985. For protecting entire regions one needs many daggers. This explains the great number of often crudely carved wooden Phurpas which can still be found in antique shops.

(8) The word Phurpa means beside many other things also 'tent peg'. In Jaeschke H. A.: 'A Tibetan-English Dictionary' we find in all the following meanings: peg, pin, nail, peg on a wall to hang up things, iron nail, wooden peg to fasten the hands of a culprit to four pegs driven into the ground, when he is to undergo the punishment of the rkyan-sin, iron instrument in the form of a short dagger, used for expelling evil spirits, and fancied to possess great power, to stick a dagger into the ground whereby the subterranean demons are kept off, to look at one with a piercing glance of the eyes, to implore a god very earnestly, the planet Jupiter, its day: Thursday.

(9) It remains uncertain so far if Padmasambhava had brought the dagger cult to Tibet from India or if he has come upon it in Tibet. In his biography (Evans-Wentz, W.Y.: 'Der geheime Pfad der grossen Befreiung', Weilheim/FRG 1972) it is expressly said that Padmasambhava had discovered (on his way to Tibet) the dagger cult, hence found it already existing. Padmasambhava can hardly be considered the inventor of the dagger cult. In a treasure text attributed to him (text 2 in the appendix to this book) one reads that he has taken the dagger doctrine from the Bhi-to-ta-ma or Vidyottama tantra.

(10) See quotation from Evans-Wentz in note 11.

(11) Until further investigation it must be left undecided whether the Phurpa cult penetrated into the Himalayas from the north or (via India and Nepal) from the south. For both possibilities legendary sources can be quoted: Nyanaponika ('Suttanipata', Konstanz 1955, p. 84) speaks of (Indian) Brahmins who wanted to avert the Buddhist king Okkaka from the teaching of the Sublime and to induce him to reintroduce (Veda) horse and human sacrfices and also "das Opfer, das man Pfeilwurf nennt" (the sacrifice called arrow throwing). In the English translation this phrase in the text has been worded 'peg throwing' (Hare, E. M.: 'Woven Cadences of Early Buddhism', p. 50). If one interprets the arrow throwing sacrifice as a form of preliminary kind of dagger cult it might have come to Tibet from India. In Padmasambhava's biography (Evans-Wentz, op. cit., p. 215) one reads however that the dagger has been rather more at home in the north: 'Eventually he (Padma) turned to the north where there was the cult of the phurbu or the magic dagger whose veneration was perfected by Padma'. According to verbal information (Lama Kunsang Dorjee, of Rikon in Switzerland) there exist in so far several lines of instruction among which one tracing the Phurpa cult back to an 'Indian king' and another according to which the Phurpa cult had been revealed by a Tibetan dakini.

(12) This fear of misuse results in the dangerous mantras (spells) in the original texts on the dagger cult attached to this book which have not been printed. They are mainly mantras of damnation the knowledge of which would not attribute much to the comprehension of the Phurpa cult.

(13) This officer was an Irishman by the name of W.F.T. O'Connor who after the Tibetan campaign was in charge of a British trade mission in Gyantse (Vide Landon, Perceval: 'Lhasa', London 1905, p. 39).

(14) Nebesky-Wojkowitz mentions in his principal work ('Oracles and Demons of Tibet', The Hague 1956) the fact that in 1952 on the occasion of the first escape of the 14th Dalai Lama he had found some knowledgable translators in his entourage in Kalimpong near the Indian-Tibetan border.

(15) This negative definition of happiness or luck, namely as the absence of misfortune, does not only exist in Asia but was also expressed by the the Greek philosopher Epicure (born in 361 B.C.) who, confronted with the impossibility to define luck or happiness, positively speaks of the absence of misfortune (letter to Menoikos).

(16) The belief in demons is not extinct in Central Europe. According to a survey of grown-up Germans (Emnid: 'Dämonenglaube', Bielefeld 1984) 13 percent of the respondents believe in the existence of spirits/demons. This percentage has remained stable in the last decade.

(17) Narrated from Grünwedel, Albert: 'Mythologie des Buddhismus in Tibet und der Mongolei', Leipzig 1900, reprint Osnabrück 1970, p. 31.

(18) The prominence of iron (meteoric iron) is frequently mentioned in literature, e. g. Brauen, Martin: 'Heinrich Harrers Impressionen aus Tibet', Innsbruck 1974, p. 208), and David-Néel, Alexandra: "Tibetan Journey", London 1936, p. 240. The hilts of the iron daggers are sometimes coated with bronze or brass: the iron of the blade must continue into the upper end of the handle which, if need be, can be ascertained by the aid of a compass. The wooden daggers are anyway made of light wood: berberis, planetree, acacia, juniper, sandalwood and the like. Nebesky-Wojkowitz (op. cit. p. 352) also mentions daggers formed of dough which are hurled against demons. So much for the realm of the visible. In the world of what is

imaginable we moreover come upon daggers made of human bones, gold, turquoise, shell-limestone, and even leather.

(19) Spectral analysis performed by the laboratory of the Thyssen Edelstahlwerke, Krefeld/Witten (FRG).

(20) The dagger practitioners normally do not classify Phurpas by outwardly discernable criteria but by invisible qualities like: Mercy Phurpa, Union Phurpa, or Emptiness Phurpa. Daggers with a lotus-like hilt are regarded more peaceful, those with a dorje-like handle as more wrathful. Basically, however, one may use any dagger type for any kind of ritual purpose as long as the Phurpa is mainly made of iron and possesses a three-edged blade (oral information by Lama Sherab Gyaltsen Amipa, of Rikon/Switzerland).

(21) The three faces of the Phurpa are mostly alike or at least similar provided the dagger comes from the folk art sector. In the case of highly artistic daggers for the use in temples the main face of the Phurpa deity (above the nose of the makara) is occasionally shaped in a peaceful expression only the two remaining faces furiously baring their teeth. It is here, though, no question of a binding rule of artistic arrangement, at most an informal custom. In the opinion of Ronge, N. Grupo ('Der Weg zum Dach der Welt', Innsbruck n. d., p. 323 ff.) the Phurpa faces were originally all more on the peaceful side and only became distorted and shaped wrathful due to Chinese influence, i. e. later.

(22) Ritual daggers are occasionally also hurled in fighting mischief causing demons. Consequently one not infrequently finds Phurpas which are broken - probably due to coming down on stones - and have later been soldered again. With old daggers the original blade has often broken off and been either entirely replaced or been coated with silver like a bad tooth.

(23) See David-Neel, Alexandra: 'Heilige und Hexer', Wiesbaden 1981, p.133.

(24) More details in Meredith, Georgette: 'The Phurba: The Use and Symbolism of the Tibetan Ritual Dagger', in History of Religions, vol. VI, no.3, Chicago 1967, and in Huntington (op. cit.).

(25) In accordance with Filchner, Wilhelm: 'Kumbum Chamba Ling', Leipzig 1933, p. 498, the Phurpa is astrologically close to the planet Jupiter. Phurpa is assigned to Thursday and on Tibetan calendars also symbolizes Thursday (see also Waddell, L. A.: 'The Buddhism of Tibet or Lamaism', London 1894, reprint Cambridge 1971, p. 455.

(26) According to Beyer, Stephan (op. cit., p. 44) the great five day Phurpa festival always starts on the eigth day of the fourth moon of the Tibetan calendar year.

(27) The sanskrit word Mandala has various meanings: round, sun disc, circle, ring, group, gang, crowd, district, area, (astronomical) track, plaything, dividers, book, section. The word yantra - erroneously often identified with mandala - however means support, blunt surgical instrument and machine. See Mylius, Klaus: 'Wörterbuch Sanskrit-Deutsch', Leipzig 1980.

(28) When trying to classify Phurpas they are best distinguished by purpose: There are daggers 1.) for worship, 2.) daggers for passive magic and 3.) daggers for active magic (exorcism). In the first category (worship) there are four sub-types: Giant-Phurpas (1 to 2 meters in height) made of sheet metal (bronze, brass) serving as temple statues; then Mandala Phurpas (30 to 70 cm in height) used to mark the centre of the mandala at solemn occasions, followed by Phurpa half-statues (15 to 60 cm), the upper part showing the winged and/or armed Phurpa deity, the lower part consisting of an (iron) blade; these half-statues serve as starting points for object-bound meditation. Next and last in this category there are full statues showing Phurpa in his anthropomorphic manifestation (normally: three faces, six arms, four legs, prajna). Phurpas for passive magic (second category) are usually made of wood (height 15 to 25 centimeters); these are planted in the ground to keep demons (hailstorms) away or they are encircling the mandala to protect it. The ritual daggers made for active magic (third category) consist (completely or partly) of iron (height: 15 to 30 centimeters); there are two sub-types: Full iron daggers (the better ones: forged

iron, the cheaper type: cast iron). Their weight should not exceed 300 to 400 grams as they are often constantly taken along by their owners. Daggers for the the use in temples, the second sub-type for active magic, often have a hilt coated with bronze or brass. These often very expensive pieces are not carried around. Therefore, their weight may exceed 400 grams considerably.

(29) See Riederer, Josef: 'Kunstwerke chemisch betrachtet', Berlin/Heidelberg/New York 1981, p. 144.

(30) The Phurpa cult was not very common among the members of the yellow-cap order (gelugpa) nor was it highly respected. Yet handling the magic dagger was not actually prohibited either. According to Lessing (op. cit., p. 272) we even find in the writings of Tsongkhapa (founder of the Gelugpa order) a text saying that the monk ought to make himself acquainted with ten capacities. In eigth place is mentioned 'the rite of accomplishing the fierce act i.e. tying down the gods with the magic nail (kila)'.

(31) In theory there is no reason why women too should not be active with the Phurpa. But there are only vague hints: the author once met a Buddhist nun of European origin on Patna airport who had lost her dagger and was rather upset about it. In the course of this meeting it had to remain open how and for what purpose she had been using the Phurpa. In the biography of the legendary dakini Yeshe Tsogyel (Dowman, Keith: 'Sky Dancer', London 1984) the dagger cult is frequently mentioned. Yeshe Tsogyel reports inter alia: 'Then I went to the Utse Pagoda where I revealed the Mandala of Dorje Phurba, and pratised Phurba's rites, until after seven days the deities of the Mandala appeared. The siddhi obtained in this practice was the power to make the enemies (demons) their own executioners'.

(32) The dagger handler must generally not stick to certain rules for his conduct of life. He may e. g. eat whatever he likes. Sexual abstinence is not prescribed (oral information by Lama Kunsang Dorje, of Rikon).

(33) Oral information by Lama Sherab Gyaltsen Amipa (Rikon), Lama Kunsang Dorjee (Rikon), and Lama Sonam Phun Tsok (Kathmandu).

(34) In Chang, C. C. (edited by Muses, C. A.): 'Esoteric Teachings of the Tibetan Tantra', n.p., 1961) one finds on p. 31 the description of an initiation for Phurpa novices. The initiation begins with the invocation of the Buddhas. The disciple is then expected to amalgamate his personality with the 'wrathful guru'. The actual initiation words (spoken by the master of the ceremony) are: 'Thus one should have faith in the teachings and lineage. O the Lotus Lord! Through his miraculous Phurba all wishes are granted and accomplishment realized. Again you should know that the Father and the Mother Guru are embodied in the Phurbu dagger. Today's initiation is called the Initiation of the Ao-rgyng (Orgyen?) Yabyum embodied in the Buddha Rdor-je-gyon-nu (Dorje Zhonnu or Phurpa) or the Elimination of Evil through the Fierce Guru with Phurba'. The novice subsequently drinks 'nectar' from a skull-cap. The master entrusts the disciple with the dagger and the other implements by pressing them on his head.

(35) In Mylius (op. cit.) 'Wörterbuch Sanskrit-Deutsch' one finds the following meanings for the word tantra: loom, warp, texture, basis, norm, rule, teaching, text-book, type of literature of magic contents, spell, means, trick, medicine, government, authority, string, row, series, and troop.

(36) Mantra means: dictum, spell, song, hymn, advice, consultation, appointment, and plan (Mylius, op. cit.).

(37) The sanskrit word mara stands for death or plague (Mylius, op. cit.). Mara is, however, also in use for (personified or not) evil which in turn is identified with ignorance but also with love, the god of love as well as the devil.

(38) The pronounciation of the mantras remains an unsolved problem in tantrism. The mantra PHAT which is quite frequent especially in the dagger cult is pronounced by the Tibetans e. g. as PHET, or PADME like PEME. These differences are not without importance because mantras can, according to the tantric teachings, only be effective whenever they are correctly articulated. But was is correct - PHAT or PHET? - cannot be unambiguously

determined. The Hindu tantrics guided by Sanskrit insist on PHAT whereas the more Tibetan oriented Buddhist tantrics maintain PHET to be correct.

(39) The word yantra (see also note 27) practically signifies a geometric figure mainly (not always) in the shape of an equilateral triangle of differing degree of reality: firstly as a triangular iron box with lid, then a picture produced by colour powder strewn on the ground, and finally in an ideated imaginary form.

(40) Mudra (fem.) amounts to ritual hand signal/mark. Mylius (op. cit.) translates this word by: seal, signet-ring, lock, stamp, print, print type, psychological) type, and mystery.

(41) The mudra of rolling the ritual dagger is interpreted in variuous ways: The dagger practitioner thereby gaining the power of all five Tathagatas or Mandala-Buddhas (personal information by N. Grupo Ronge, of Königswinter/FRG). Stein writes in this context: 'Le sadhana de Phur-pa comporte le roulement du phurbu entre les dix doigts des deux mains dans lesquelles on imagine les divinités masculines et féminines en accouplement produisant le bodhicitta (secret)'. (The Phurpa sadhana contains the rolling of the dagger between the ten fingers of both hands in which one imagines the masculin and feminin deities mating to beget the bodhicitta; secret), see Stein, R. A.: 'A propos des documents anciens relatifs au Phur-bu (Kila)', Proceedings of the Csoma de Körös Memorial Symposium, Bibliotheca Orientalis Hungarica, vol. XXIII, Budapest 1978, p. 481. According to Lama Sherab Gyaltsen Amipa, of Rikon, the dagger rolling mudra 'sets the energy current against mara in motion'.

(42) On the one hand the simple people are just afraid of the incalculability especially the remote effect of the dagger forces. On the other hand the dagger doctrine raises dogmatic problems: are the demons (sentient beings) actually 'killed' (in Tibetan: bsad) or are they 'liberated' (Tibetan: sgrol) and removed to a 'Buddha land'? In the Tibetan texts on the Phurpa cult it unambiguously says 'bsad' (kill). The word sgrol (liberate) is also in use (in an euphemistic sense?). Supposing it should read 'liberate' really then one would have to fancy the liberation roughly like this: the dagger practitioner sucks the adverse demon up with his Phurpa. The god-dagger would thus possess the power to free the demon from its bad karma and to release it into a better reincarnation. By some information, though slightly unprecise, the dagger handler is supposed to drive the demon caught in the yantra through a stupa (ideated or drawn on paper) the purifying power of which should also secure a better rebirth for the demon.

(43) Quoted in accordance with Beyer, Stephan, op. cit., p. 352.

(44) Ever since Buddhism was confronted with the tantra cult the question has obviously been discussed whether certain tantric practices like the ritual murder sgrol-ba (but also the ritual intercourse sbyor-ba) are compatible with the Buddhist doctrine. The Buddhist teacher Dipamkarasrijnana (Atisa) in 1042 travelled for clarifying this complex of questions from India (Bengal) upon request to Tibet. The issue in detail was whether the ritual killing of a person possessed by evil could be regarded as an act of 'special compassion' or if this would invariably remain a deadly sin (parajika). This discussion was caused by the ritual slaying of the non-Buddhist Tibetan king Glan-dar-ma by a Buddhist believer. This doctrine of the permissible ritual killing for special compassion, tinged by tantrism, seems to have been widespread in Tibet at least at the time of Atisa, especially as a justification ideology of Buddhist gangs of robbers. Even nowadays people still subscribe to this here and there - particularly in the frame-work of the Phurpa cult. For further information see Ruegg, D. S.: 'Deux problèmes d'exégèse et de pratique tantrique selon Dipamkarasrijnana...' in 'Taoist and Tantric Studies in Honour of R.A. Stein', Brussels 1984, p. 212.

(45) At the occasion of an instruction granted by the Venerable Khenpo Rinpoche Yeshe Chödar, of Menton (France) in Huy-Tihange (Belgium) the author was informed that 'killing' and 'liberating' are no contradiction: Provided that the Phurpa practitioner performs the ritual the authentic way the demon (the life-demon of a human being) is killed and liberated at the same moment. Physical death and spiritual liberation have to be

considered as a unity. But if the practitioner follows a non-authentic line of instruction it might happen that the demon (the person) is just dead and not liberated. It seems, therefore, likely that a sentient being, accidentally or not, can be thrown out of the circle of rebirth during a Phurpa ceremony.

(46) These six rules represent a compilation by the author based on not attributable personal information but also on Huntington (op. cit., p. 4).

(47) This annual dagger procession is mentioned inter alia in Ferrari, Alfonsa: 'Mk'yen Brtse's Guide to the Holy Places of Central Tibet', Rome 1958, p. 100: 'This magic dagger (p'ur bu) is the object of great veneration in Tibet. People are allowed to touch it only once a year after the Dalai Lama, to whom it is brought in procession during the feast of smon lam. Touching the p'ur bu protects against evil spirits. The tradition relates that this wonderful dagger arrived flying from India and fell upon a hill near Sera (monastery)'.

(48) With the reference to the Buddha land it is possibly alluded that the demon afterwards is neither dead nor reborn.

(49) The hailmaster of His Holiness the 14th Dalai Lama is described and depicted with dagger in Lehmann, Peter-Hannes: 'Tibet', Hamburg 1981, p. 226-7. Lehmann writes the Dalai Lama had brought his weather maker with him to Ladakh on the occasion of a big kalachakra inauguration. His task was to protect the many participants in the open-air event from storm and rain and this by the aid of the dagger and the bone trumpet.

(50) In danced mystery plays those monks acting as the defenders of the Buddhist doctrine occasionally hold Phurpas in their hands. They also trample down the enemies of Buddhism (demons) or knife an effigy, a linga made of dough. See Evans-Wenz, W. Y.: 'Yoga und die Geheimlehren Tibets, München-Planegg 1937, p. 201 ff.

(51) Mentioned in Hermanns, Matthias: 'Das Nationalepos der Tibeter Gling König Gesar', Regensburg 1965.

(52) A description of the use of the Phurpa in speedwalking may be found in David-Néel, Alexandra: 'Heilige und Hexer', Wiesbaden 1981 (revised edition), p. 169 ff.

(53) See Kawaguchi, Ekai: 'Three Years in Tibet', Madras/Benares 1909, reprint New Delhi 1979, p. 275.

(54) Reported inter alia in Lewiston, David: 'Tibetan Buddhism Shedur: A Ghost Exorcism Ritual', record cover, Explorer Series, H-7208, New York 1978.

(55) Narrated in accordance with Evans-Wentz, W. Y.: 'Der geheime Pfad der grossen Befreiung', op. cit.

(56) One occasionally finds allusions to Phurpa rituals - within this basic pattern - having been performed in various ways. Thus e. g. in a Tibetan travel-guide of the 19th century it is expressly mentioned where the dagger cult of Orgyen Rinpoche's method is practised. From this one is tempted to conclude that at least during the time this travel guide was written also other forms of the Phurpa cult might have been common. The text reads as follows: 'Coming from a valley between Ban Pa and mKar c'u after having crossed a snowy pass, at the head of the Mon Kh'ru valley, there is a remarkable place called Ne rin sen ge rdsom gsum in Mon K'a, where the ceremony of the p'ur pa according to the method of Orgyen Rinpo'ce is performed' (Ferrari, Alfonsa, op. cit., p. 56).

(57) Music is no prerequisite in the Phurpa cult. But if the ritual is accompanied by music mainly the big handle drum, the shaking drum, big brass cimbals, bone trumpets, and hand bells are used. Phurpa music has been recorded by Jest and Lewiston (see list of sources).

(58) Oral information by Lama Sherab Gyaltsen Amipa, of Rikon.

(59) See Nebesky-Wojkowitz, Rene de: 'Oracles and Demons of Tibet', The Hague 1956, reprint Graz 1975, p. 482.

(60) For the prominence of mustard seed one cannot find a really comprehensible explanation. It must presumably be traced back to the fact that mustard seed grains are very small and at the same time big plants spring from them. This cause and effect relation is mentioned in the New Testament no less than four times (Math. 13.31 and 17.20, Mark 4.31 and Luke 13.19). In Mathew 13.31 it says: 'Another parable He (Jesus) put before them and said: The kingdom of heaven is like a mustard grain which a man took and sowed it on a field which is the smallest among all seeds. But if it grows up it will be the biggest under the cabbage (the cabbage types) and becomes a tree so that the birds of the sky come and live under its branches'. In Math. 17.20 it says: 'Verily I say unto you: If your belief be like a mustard grain you may say to this mountain: lift yourself off thereto! So it will rise; and nothing will be impossible to you'.

(61) See Nebesky-Wojkowitz, op. cit., p. 483.

(62) The word linga means: mark, symptom, phallus, (grammatical) gender, fine body, and idol (Mylius, op. cit., p. 412).

(63) In Filchner, Wilhelm: 'Kumbum Dschamba Ling', Leipzig 1933, p. 293, the lingas in the form of dough pictures are mentioned as follows: 'If the tormas (dough pictures) are supposed to be traps... the Lamas summon the evil spirits and force them into the tormas... But once detained in the tormas they remain prisoners since the 'front garden' (the immediate vicinity of the dough pictures) is bristling with a rampart of small magic daggers preventing the demons from getting away'.

(64) Quoted according to Beyer, Stephan, op. cit., p. 316.

(65) Mentioned in Evans-Wentz, W.Y.: 'Yoga und die Geheimlehren Tibets', (op. cit., p. 201) here with reference to the Chöd ritual.

(66) Narrated according to Landon, Perceval: 'Lhasa', London 1905, and Waddell, L.A.: 'Lhasa and its Mysteries', London 1905.

(67) The meaning of the spoken text is not what primarily matters. What is decisive is the internality in consequence of the perpetual repetition of the words once chosen. The effect of such 'heart's prayer' has been very impressively described by an anonymous Christian mystic (von Walter, Reinhold, editor: 'Aufrichtige Erzählungen eines russischen Pilgers', Freiburg im Breisgau 1959).

(68) So called in Stein, R.A.: 'A propos des documents...', op. cit., p.431.

(69 Quoted in accordance to Beyer, Stephan (op. cit. p. 134) and Ruegg, D.S. 'The Life of Bu-ston Rinpoche', Rome 1966.

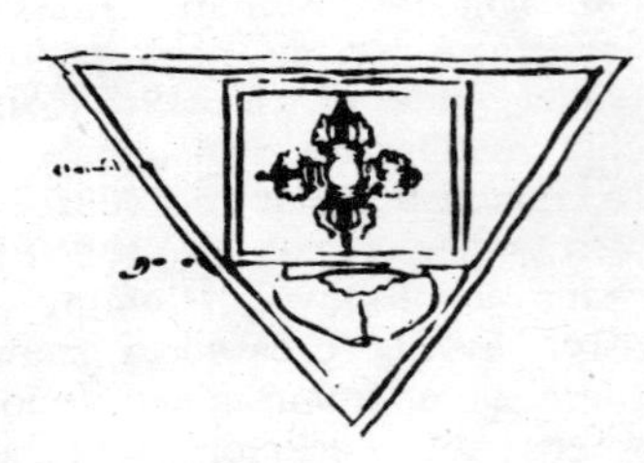

Sources

BOOKS

BEYER, Stephan: "The Cult of Tara", Berkeley/London 1973

BHARATI, A.: "The Tantric Tradition", London 1965.

BISCHOFF, F.A. and HARTMANN, Ch.: "Padmasambhava's Invention of the Phurpa", Etudes Tibetaines, Paris 1971.

BRAUEN, Martin: "Heinrich Harrers Impressionen aus Tibet", Innsbruck 1974.

CANTWELL, Cathy: "Tibetan Buddhist Ritual in a Refugee Monastery", The Tibet Journal, Autumn 1985, Dharamsala, India.

CHANG, C.C. and MUSES, C.A.: "Esoteric Teachings of the Tibetan Tantras", n.p., 1961.

DAS, Sarat Chandra: "A Short Description of the Phurpa", in Journal of the Buddhist Society, IV, 1896, p. 5.

DAVID-NEEL, Alexandra: "Heilige und Hexer", Leipzig 1936.

DAVID-NEEL, Alexandra: "Tibetan Journey", London 1936.

DOWMAN, Keith (translator): "Sky Dancer", London 1984.

EVANS-WENTZ, W.Y.: "Der geheime Pfad der grossen'Befreiung", Weilheim 1972.

EVANS-WENTZ, W.Y.: "Yoga und die Geheimlehren Tibets", München-Planegg 1937.

FERRARI, Alfonsa: "Mk'yen Brtse's Guide to the Holy Places of Central Tibet", Roma 1958.

FILCHNER, W.: "Kumbum Dschamba Ling", Leipzig 1933.

GRÜNWEDEL, Albert: "Mythologie des Buddhismus in Tibet und der Mongolei", Leipzig 1900.

HERMANNS, Matthias: "Das Nationalepos der Tibeter Gling König Gesar", Regensburg 1965.

HELLER, Amy: "Rkyal 'Bud, Notes on an Early Tibetan Ritual", in Aziz, B. and Kapstein, M. (editors): "Sounddings in Tibetan Civilisation" (Proceedings of the 1982 Seminar of the International Association for Tibetan Studies), New Delhi 1985.

HELLER, Amy: "Early Textual Sources for the Cult of Beg-ce", Proceedings 1985 of the International Association for Tibetan Studies, Munich 1986, publication in progress.

HOFFMANN, H.: "La religione Bon tibetana", Roma 1943.

HOFFMANN, H.: "The Religions of Tibet", New York 1961.

HUMMEL, Siegbert: "Der lamaistische Ritualdolch (Phurbu) und die altorientalischen Nagelmenschen", Asiatische Studien, pp. 41-51, Bern 1952.

HUMMEL, S.: "Vajrakila", Wiss. Z. Univ. Halle, 22, 1972.

HUMMEL, S.: "Noch einmal Vajrakila", Wiss. Z. Univ. Halle, 23, 1974.

HUNTINGTON, John C.: "The Phur-pa - Tibetan Ritual Daggers", Ascona 1975.
KIPPENBERG, Hans G. und LUCHESI, Brigitte (editors): "Magie - die sozialwissenschaftliche Kontroverse über das Verstehen fremden Denkens", Frankfurt 1978.
KLAUS: Chr.: "Schutz vor Naturgewalten", Asiatische Forschung, Vol. 37, p. 310, Wiesbaden 1985.
LANDON, Perceval: "Lhasa", London 1905.
LAUF, Detlev Ingo: "Über die Gottheiten des magischen Dolches Vajrakila", in A. Körösi Csoma Sandor Intézet Közlemenyei, Budapest 1974.
LEHMANN, Peter-Hannes: "Tibet", Hamburg 1981.
LESSING, F.D.: Collected Essays on Lamaism and Chinese Symbolism", Taipei 1976.
LESSING, F.D.: "Introduction to Buddhist Tantric Systems", den Haag 1968.
LHALUNGPA, Lobsang P.: "Tibetan Music", in A. Körösi Csoma Sandor Intézet Közlemenyei, Budapest 1974.
MARCOTTY, Thomas: "The Way-Music", Lugano 1980.
MEREDITH, Georgette: "The Phurbu: The Use and Symbolism of the Tibetan Magic Dagger", in History of Religions, Vol. VI, no. 3, Chicago 1967.
MYLIUS, K.: "Wörterbuch Sanskrit-Deutsch", Leipzig 1980.
NEBESKY-WOJKOWITZ, René de: "Die tibetische Bön Religion", Archiv für Völkerkunde, Vol. II, Wien 1947.
NEBESKY-WOJKOWITZ, René de: "Oracles and Demons+of Tibet", den Haag 1956.
NOELLE-NEUMANN, Elisabeth: "Politik und Glück", in Baier, Horst (editor): "Freiheit und Sachzwang - Beiträge zu Ehren Helmut Schelskys", Opladen, n.d.
NYANAPONIKA (translator): "Sutta-Nipata", Konstanz 1955.
PETZOLDT, Leander (editor): "Magie und Religion, Beiträge zu einer Theorie der Magie", Darmstadt 1978.
ROCK, J.F.: " The Amnye Ma-Chhen Range", Roma 1956.
ROERICH, G.N.: "The Blue Annals", Vol. 1, Calcutta 1949.
RONGE, N. Gonpo: "Kunst und Stil in Tibet", in MÜLLER, Claudius C. and RAUNIG, Walter (editors): "Auf dem Dach der Welt", Innsbruck, n.d.
RUEGG, D.S.: "The Life of Buston Rinpoche", Roma 1966.
RUEGG, D.S.: "Deux problêmes d'exêgese et de pratique tantrique selon Dipamkarasrijnana et le Paindapatika de Yavadvipa/Suvarnadvipa" in "Tantric and Taoist Studies in Honour of R. A. Stein", p. 212, Bruxelles 1981.
SCHLAGINTWEIT, Emile de: "Le Bouddhisme au Tibet", in Annales du Musêe Guimet, Lyon 1881.
SCHUMANN, Hans Wolfgang: "Buddhismus - Stifter, Schulen und Systeme", Olten 1976.
SCHUMANN, Hans Wolfgang: "Buddhistische Bilderwelt, Pantheon und Symbolik tibetisch-nepalischer Drucke - ein ikonographisches Handbuch des Mahayana-Buddhismus", Köln 1986.
STEIN, R. A.: "Le linga des danses masquêes lamaiques et la theorie des âmes", in Liebenthal Festschrift, p. 200, Santinikitan 1957.

STEIN, R. A.: "A propos des documents anciens relatifs au Phur-bu (Kila)", Memorial Symposium, Bibliotheca+Orientalis Hungarica, Vol XXIII, p. 427, Budapest 1978.

TUCCI, Giuseppe: "Tibetan Painted Scrolls", Roma 1949.

UHLIG, H.: "Tantrische Kunst des Buddhismus", Berlin, Frankfurt, Wien 1981.

WADDELL, L.A.: "Lamaism in Sikkhim", London 1894, Reprint New Delhi 1973.

WADDELL, L.A.: "The Buddhism of Tibet or Lamaism", Cambridge 1894.

WADDELL, L.A.: "Lhasa and its Mysteries", London 1905, Reprint Taipei 1972.

WALTER, Reinhold von (editor): "Aufrichtige Erzählungen eines russischen Pilgers", Freiburg i. Br. 1959.

TIBETAN SOURCES

PHUR PA Texts of the byan-gter Tradition, Dalhousie 1977.

PHUR PA DRIL SGRUB reprint (Staatsbibliothek München, 4* L. tibet 6 v-75).

PHUR PA YAN GSAN BLA MED DON GYI SNIN PO LAS RGYAB CHOS SMAD LAS DUG PHUR NAG PO'I MTSHON CHA LAS KYI 'KHOR LO, copied manuscript ascribed to RATNA-GLIN-PA (15th century).

TWO RARE VAJRAKILA TEACHINGS (Padmasambhava?), Staatsbibliothek München, 2* L. tibet. 13 r.

KANJUR, Peking Edition, Vol. 3, no. 78 ("Vajrakilaya...") p. 154-4-8; and Vol. 10, no. 467 ("Vajramantra..."), p. 186-4-4.

RECORDS

JEST, C.: "Tibet-Nepal", Disque BAM, LD 104, Paris 1966.

LEWISTON, David: "Tibetan Buddhism - Shedur: A Ghost Exorcism Ritual", Explorer Series, H-72081, New York 1978.

PICTURES

The photos in this book have been taken by the author if not stated otherwise. Objects: Tibet collection Marcotty. The xylographic design on page 80 is taken from Huntington, John C.: "The Phur-pa - Tibetan Ritual Daggers" with kind permission of the author. The remaining Tibetan wood engravings are reproduced from Waddell, L.A.: "The Buddhism of Tibet or Lamaism" with the exception of the picture on page 86 which was bought on a Tibetan market in Nepal. The ink drawings are taken from Ratnaglin-pa's manual for Phurpa practitioners.